Elsie's Biscuits

Simple Stories of Me, My Mother, and Food

by Laurey Masterton

To Lucinda, who told me what to do—and was right.

To Heather, who continues to tell me to send it in.

And to Chris, no matter what.

Designed by Pam Ruatto

ISBN: 978-0-9790957-6-4

Cover photo by Aubrey P. Janion
Back cover photo by Emily Weber Thome

Laurey C. Masterton
Laurey's: Catering & Gourmet Comfort Food
67 Biltmore Avenue
Asheville, NC 28801

www.Laureysyum.com

Contents

Prologue

The first week of February was *not* a quiet week in Asheville, my adopted home town. Garrison Keillor and members of his *Prairie Home Companion* gang came here on a Monday night to do a show. Oh my, what a night it was!

First of all, let me go on record as saying that I have been a huge Garrison fan since that show started being broadcast—how ever many years ago that was.

One time, a number of years ago, right in the middle of what was supposed to be an extended mountain-climbing excursion in the Bugaboo Mountains of British Columbia, I decided that I did not want to die climbing and that, frankly, the previous day's nineteen-hour climbing excursion was going to be my last. I calculated that, if we left that moment and drove nonstop, we could be in St. Paul in time for the Saturday live broadcast of *A Prairie Home Companion*. My climbing partner/girlfriend grudgingly agreed to go (she wanted to stay and climb more) and so we drove, stopping only for gas and minimal sleep, until we reached the box office—just a couple of hours before the show. We got put on the waiting list and managed to squeak in at the *very* last minute. My heart still pounds remembering standing in that line, hoping, hoping, hoping we would make it off the waiting list and into seats.

That show was glorious. I sank into the stories. Loved the music. And basked in the evening, thrilled, most of all, to be far away from those treacherous rocks. I never looked back.

All this came rushing back the other night when we got to provide the food for the morning, noon, and evening meals of *A Prairie Home Companion*'s Asheville show for our public broadcasting radio station, WCQS. Jon, our delivery driver, did a full day's work shuttling back and forth with coffee, fresh cookies, and such. It was my day off, but, curious, I went by in the midafternoon to check on things and happened to walk by Garrison's dressing room.

The door was open.

He was there.

I skidded to a stop.

"Hi! I'm *so* glad you're here!!! My name is Laurey and we're cooking dinner for you tonight!" I blurted out.

"Hello," Garrison looked up. I was a nervous wreck! He *is* my hero!

"I was just up your way on a dog-sledding trip," I said. Boy, did I sound nervous!

"Um hmm . . ."

We had a conversation of sorts. Politics, dogs, food, this and that.

"This might just be my lucky day," I stammered. Was my voice really shaking? Sheesh!

"Oh, why's that?" he looked at me over his glasses. He probably gets this all the time, I scolded myself.

"Well, I have been working on a book and today is the day the agent will receive it. She told me she'd read it this week and let me know what she thought next week. I'm pretty excited about the whole thing."

"What kind of book is it?" Garrison asked.

"It's called *Elsie's Biscuits: Simple Stories of Me, My Mother, and Food*," I said, still nervous.

"Hmm . . . I see." Right, I thought, probably *everyone* who talks to him has a book in the works. Why am I rattling on?

"Is any of it dark?" he asked.

Great question! I thought. "Dark? Yes," I said. "there are dark parts."

"Good. It's good if some of it is dark."

I nodded.

"Now, your name, is that L-A-U-R-I-E?" he spelled.

"No, L-A-U-R-E-Y," I spelled back, "like the show *Oklahoma*. The protagonist's name was spelled that way and my father was reading a review of the show while my mother was in the delivery room."

"Oh, I see," he said.

"And Masterton is Scottish. It comes from 'master of the town,' or something like that," I continued. "Well, nice talking to you. I need to run now." I didn't, but I was feeling stupid.

I left the theater, wandered around town, dazed at my conversation. Garrison Keillor!!! I floated all afternoon, thrilled. Boy, so many years ago I had gone so far out of my way to see him and—wow—I had just talked to my hero. Wow, wow, wow.

And then it was time for the show. What a show! The sound was amazing, the music blissful. Stories flowed. The time flew.

"Okay," said Garrison, "everybody stand up. It's time for intermission. Leave if you need to, but for all the rest of you, let's all just sing together, shall we? I mean, how often do you get to sing together in a big room with all these people?"

So we all sang. What fun! How rich we sounded!

"And now," he said after we'd all sung for a long time, "let's do one more song. I'd like to dedicate this one to," he paused dramatically, "Laurey Masterton. She made our dinner tonight, which is why the music sounds so good. So," he continued without explaining why, "let's all sing 'Oklahoma.'"

And then we—me and everyone else, all 2,400 of us (give or take)—sang.

"O-K-L-A-H-O-M-A. Oklahoma!!!!"

Can you imagine?

I still can't. Wow. Wow. Wow.

P.S. The agent called right when she said she would, and said that yes, she *did* want to work with me. So it looks like it *was* my lucky day, in so very many ways.

Introduction

Both my parents died the year I was twelve.

That's not exactly an experience I would recommend for an easy childhood, but it is also not the worst. The truth is, I had twelve incredibly golden years before things came crashing in around me. And, now that I look back, things have worked out pretty well, even with such a horrendous jolt that year.

I grew up in a wonderful Inn in the mountains of Vermont. I watched my mother and father and absorbed everything I saw, and now I run my own place in the mountains of North Carolina. It's not an Inn, but I do live my life in and around food, inspired by what my parents did with their lives. I think my parents would have been pleased.

My mother told stories of how things were for her. She often sent them to her mother who would sigh and say, "Oh, Elsie, this is wonderful! Send it in!" Mama never said whom to send these stories to, but eventually, once my mother collected enough, she did send them in and, to her delight, they were published in the first of five books she wrote—all about Blueberry Hill, the Inn in Vermont.

As I've built my life, I have collected stories, too. Periodically I send them to my sisters, who say, "Oh, Laurey, *this* one is great! Send it in!" So, finally, I did.

These, then, are my stories of how it has been for me.

Laurey Masterton
July 2006

Chapter One

Dolly's Beef Stroganoff

 I was sixteen days old when my mother curdled Dolly Arnold's Beef Stroganoff. It was going to be served at her annual gathering for the prominent ladies in town—a group of some seventy-five. It was an unseasonably hot Memorial Day and, when my mother added the sour cream, the beef was too hot and the whole mess boiled and then separated and was, in short, unusable.

This was not the first party my mother had cooked for Dolly, nor was it the first time she'd made Beef Stroganoff. But it was the first time it had ever been that hot on Memorial Day weekend. Usually late May and early June in Vermont were mild. It would not have been unusual to have had to wear a light sweater during the day at that time of year, and at night it was essential.

My parents were in the habit of telling guests to bring a light jacket or sweater even if they came to visit Blueberry Hill in July. By the time I was born, we had room for about sixteen guests if we had a full house, though a full house was rare. There was "Nothing Whatever To Do" at Blueberry Hill. No social director. No schedule of activities. No list of things that a person could fill one's day with. My parents wanted it that way. When they were putting the place together—once they realized that their dream of owning a ski area was not going to work and they were creating a country inn—they were quite intentional about how it would be. "Nothing Whatever To Do," they decided, was the best possible way an Inn could be.

"Let's serve Lucullan Food," they said, Lucullus being a Roman general who loved fine food. My parents knew good food, having dined out often during the days when my father was a successful New York attorney and my mother was a secretary for a prominent orthopedic surgeon, also in the city. My father knew fine words. He found this word when they were looking for the right description for their food. Pulled it out. Suggested it. And they adopted it, deciding that was the kind of food they wanted to serve at their Inn.

My mother had not known how to cook when she moved to Vermont. My father had not known how to build a ski area. But in a moment of passion he had purchased a chunk of land that had, the ad in the *New York Herald Tribune* said, a mountain. He hired some fellows, cut the trees, and built a ski area. Well before the time of artificial snow-making, the ski area failed. It *did* snow, just not at the right time. For example, it snowed on Monday. The men and my father would get out there on Tuesday and Wednesday and hand pack the slopes. (This means they tromped up and down each trail, stamping a path for skiers to use.) And then, inevitably, it would rain on Thursday, ruining the possibility of a weekend of skiing. Alternatively, it would snow so much that no one could manage to get up The Big Hill from town. The slopes, loaded with snow, would sit, packed and ready, but very empty.

Someone had to cook for the men; someone had to figure out how to set up a snack area for the skiers. My father was busy packing the slopes. My mother, left at home all day long with one and then two babies, had to learn how to cook. Someone had to. She became a student of whatever cookbooks she could find at the library and discovered that not only was she an adequate cook, she actually was very good at it. Of course, the men were pretty hungry after spending all that time out cutting trees and packing the ski slopes and probably would have eaten anything. But still, she could tell that she was good. After all, she knew what good food was from living well in New York City, which was not, she knew, the same as being able to cook it. But her mother was a very good cook and my mother realized that she had it in her blood too.

Yes, she realized, she could cook.

When the ski area flopped after too many years of poor snow, my parents were left with a thousand acres of beautiful land, a big old farmhouse, and a couple of barns. There were three children by then. There was no turning back.

"You ought to open up an Inn," people said. "This is a beautiful spot. You ought to give it a shot."

They didn't have much of a choice. The nest egg they'd had a few years ago was gone. The ski area was not working. They had been gone too long to go back to New York. Their life was in Vermont, but how they were going to make it was not clear.

"Yes, open up an Inn," their friends said. "Elsie, you can cook, and John, well, John can be the host."

Which is what they did.

My father, who had learned some carpentry from building the ski area, made the old woodshed right behind the main part of the old farmhouse into guest rooms. The single bathroom upstairs in the main house was divided and became a couple of smaller bathrooms. My parents turned the biggest room into a dining room and, not having any money for more elaborate decoration, painted recipes on the walls in the old kitchen to hide the cracks in the plaster. They put an ad in *The Saturday Review*: "Lucullan Food. *Nothing Whatever to Do*."

A single guest came. And then another. My mother cooked. My father, gracious, hosted and served the guests.

My mother wrote long letters to her mother, telling her in great detail all about the day-to-day woes and triumphs of their venture. I have one letter that is eight pages long, single spaced, describing every bit of the very first weekend when guests came to the Inn. "Mama," my mother wrote, "we FINALLY have guests coming this weekend. A whole ski club from New Jersey. I have been running around borrowing beds and sheets and blankets from everyone all over Goshen. 45 people, Mama! Imagine that?!" There are lists of all the groceries she bought, the responses to the meals, the fun the guests all had. In the letter, my mother is proud, exhilarated. It is an exciting letter for me to read now. Yet reading it makes me feel tired and sad, knowing about all that was to come at her.

"Oh Elsie," Mama wrote back, "this is wonderful! I think you should send it in!"

Mama always told my mother to "send it in," and from her silly poems in first grade, my mother had done what her mother said to do, sending in her jottings to the local newspaper. I have my mother's diaries, complete with newspaper clippings of those printed poems. So, when Mama told my mother to send it in, she did. And the person she sent it to at Crown Publishers liked what she sent. The first book was on its way to being published: stories of the beginning of the Inn, complete with her initial recipes.

I appear at the very end of this first book, called *Nothing Whatever to Do*, in the last paragraph of the last chapter, which is titled, "The Most Considerate Children in the World." My two older sisters Lucinda and Heather and I were "considerate" because we were all born off-season, coming either before or after the rush of summer visitors to the Inn. In that last paragraph I am asleep in a laundry basket in the den of the Inn, sleeping through Dolly Arnold's party.

Oh, if you are wondering what happened with the ruined Beef Stroganoff: my mother made some urgent phone calls to the butcher in town who, even though it was the Sunday of Memorial Day weekend, went in to work, cut up a whole new round of beef, gathered sour cream and onions, packed it all up, and sent it up to Blueberry Hill with Lyle's Taxi Service. My mother and father cooked a whole new batch of Stroganoff, and Dolly's seventy-five guests enjoyed their meal, unaware that anything unusual had happened.

My mother went on to write three cookbooks and one other book of stories about the Inn, but that is a longer story all by itself. For now, let's stop with me asleep in the laundry basket while the Beef Stroganoff was served.

I think about being sixteen days old and attending my very first catered party. When I stop to think about how I got where I am now, I realize I have been gearing up for the kind of work I am now doing for my entire life, including telling the stories of what happened along the way.

Dolly's Beef Stroganoff
The Recipe

In case you'd like to try the Beef Stroganoff, here's my mother's recipe. (By the way, whenever I include one of my mother's recipes, I record it just as she wrote it.) Of course, diets and eating plans are different now than they were in the late 1950s. If you feel like changing things around, cutting back on the fat, for instance, well, that's up to you. I'd say just follow the recipe—and don't eat too much!

Serves 6

The ingredients:

2 pounds round steak
1 clove garlic
2 tablespoons flour
3 teaspoons salt
¼ teaspoon pepper
granulated garlic (not garlic salt or garlic powder)

1 large onion
1 chicken bouillon cube
1 pound fresh mushrooms
1 cup sour cream
1 teaspoon sugar (optional)

Here's what you do: (This is what I say, this "here's what you do" phrase. I like it, so I've decided to start each recipe, even my mother's, with these words.)

Rub steak on both sides with a cut clove of garlic. Pound into it a mixture of flour, salt, and pepper. Cut meat, against the grain, into thin strips about 2 inches long. Peel the onion and cut it small. In a heavy frying pan or kettle with a cover, brown the onion in some of the trimmings of beef fat. Remove onion with slotted spoon. Brown the meat quickly in the same fat. Return onion to pan with meat. Cover tightly and let simmer 15 minutes over very low heat. The meat should be quite tender. If you are using a lesser cut of meat, it will take a little longer, so be sure to remove a piece and take a bite at this point.

Dissolve chicken bouillon cube in 1 cup water. Slice the mushrooms. Add bouillon and mushrooms to the meat, cover tightly, and simmer until mushrooms are just beginning to brown, about 10 minutes. Uncover. Be sure meat and mushrooms are tender. Remove from heat and allow to cool to room temperature.

Just before serving, stir in the sour cream, also at room temperature. The sour cream will curdle if it is too cold or if the meat is too hot.

Taste for seasoning, and add salt, pepper, and a little granulated garlic if you feel like it. If you want it a little more interesting, add 1 teaspoon of sugar. It won't taste sweet; just extra good.

Chapter Two

Shrimp Tempura

 I have the pot my mother used to cook Shrimp Tempura. I have cooked in it but now, to tell the truth, it just sits next to my desk, propping up some of my favorite books and reminding me of my mother and the Inn and that time of my life.

We served Shrimp Tempura every single night at Blueberry Hill. It was so popular that every time my mother tried to make something new, the regulars protested. Finally my mother gave in. After a time she stopped trying anything else.

Shrimp Tempura with John's Dunk Sauce was one of the few things which I, still a child, was allowed to serve. Working in the dining room was off-limits to an eight-year-old, though I was sure I could serve as well as any of the college girls we hired. But Shrimp Tempura was served to the guests when they were still sitting in the den or the living room waiting to be invited in for dinner, so I was allowed to help.

I passed napkins to the guests and Heather, following behind, gave each guest a small dish, a "monkey dish" my mother called it, though I never knew why. It did not look like a monkey to me, just like a little bowl. Who ever came up with "monkey?" I wondered. My mother stayed in the kitchen cooking the shrimp.

This pot of hers is black. A cast-iron pot, it has a handle and had, at one point, a basket that fit inside. My mother never used the basket, preferring to lift the cooked shrimp with a slotted spoon.

Thirty minutes before the guests arrived, my mother filled the pot with peanut oil and turned on the gas on her Magic Chef stove. She waited until most everyone had arrived and then she quickly whisked an egg with some milk and then blended that mixture into flour, salt, and baking powder. Stirred together just until barely combined, this simple batter became her nightly magic.

The college girls who worked as our summer staff spent the afternoon helping prepare the dinner. Five or six of them stayed with us through the summer each year, cleaning guest rooms, working in the kitchen, serving the dinners. I hovered as close as possible, absorbing their every move, memorizing their jokes, trying to work myself into their very center. To me, nothing was better than being in the heart of the kitchen, right in the middle of this activity.

The shrimp needed to be peeled and deveined. We had a hard red plastic pointed thing that the girls used to peel and devein the shrimp, a job that was off-limits to me. Interestingly, now that I make Shrimp Tempura I buy shrimp that are already peeled because we make so many that it would take many hours to get the shells off them all. I guess my mother couldn't get them that way—what a lot of time it would have saved.

Shrimp Tempura was served with my father's dipping sauce. John's Dunk Sauce, we said. My father's only food invention, it went perfectly with my mother's shrimp. It started like a Russian salad dressing but he'd jazzed it up with horseradish and vinegar.

When the guests were all seated on couches in our front rooms, my mother started cooking. She'd take one shrimp by the tail, dip it into the batter, and then drop it into the hot oil. She had a trick for knowing if the oil was hot enough. When she turned on the gas burner she put a "strike anywhere" kitchen match into the pot with the oil. And when the oil reached the right temperature, the match ignited. (You have to use a "strike anywhere" match or it won't work. Trust me, I've found this out the hard way!)

"I always wondered why the whole pot didn't explode," Heather said when I told her I was writing about Shrimp Tempura. "Every night she dropped in that match, and every night I expected the whole thing to blow up, but of course it never did."

My mother's pot held about four shrimp at a time. We had room for about twenty guests for dinner. So when the four shrimp had turned a light golden fluff my mother took them out of the oil with her slotted spoon, patted them on a paper towel, and then dunked four more into the batter, dropping them into the oil. Dip, drop, spoon, pat. Dip, drop, spoon, pat. Watching her was comforting. Regular. Familiar. She never hurried, never seemed rushed. Dip, drop, spoon, pat.

Lucinda—being twelve and sophisticated—had what I considered to be the great good fortune of being the one to take the shrimp out to the guests.

"Just dunk one into the Dunk Sauce," she explained, "and leave the tail in your little monkey dish." The guests, having heard about the shrimp, did as they were told, smiling at my sister. I stood at the foot of the stairs just outside the den, hovering, knowing that I could do this job. I was able to do much more than pass out napkins, if they'd only let me.

My mother, in the kitchen, kept cooking.

I have a series of pictures of my mother cooking Shrimp Tempura with the pot that is now mine. My father hovers nearby, smiling and handsome. This is one of the photographs taken for one of their many publicity events that they did in support of their cookbooks. In the first picture, my mother is swirling the shrimp in the batter. In the next, she is taking the perfect puff out of the oil. And in the third, she is feeding it to my father.

I don't have any wedding pictures of my parents, so I'm not even sure if they had a cake, but this is a very good stand-in, the two of them looking so happy, cooking and being with each other. They are feeding each other, showing crinkles of a smile, looking into each other's eyes. There is a ritual quality to these pictures.

Through the years at the Inn there were so many shrimp. And in those pictures it is easy to see that my parents were so much in love. They showed it by making and eating Shrimp Tempura. And yes, they told each other how much they loved each other.

"I love you, Sweetie Pie," she seemed to say, dropping another shrimp in her pot.

Even after forty years, my mother's Shrimp Tempura continues to be a classic. Just the other night I served dinner to 100 guests. We had three other very nice hors d'oeuvres, but once I started cooking the shrimp, the guests wanted nothing to do with anything else. I find it amazing that this recipe is still the most favorite thing I serve.

Now I sit and look at this pot. When my half sister, a child of my father's first marriage, gave it to me ("Say, I thought you might want this. It's been gathering dust in the barn all these years"), I carried it around with me, moving it from room to room, cooking in it, holding onto the handle as if it could bring me closer to my mother. But in fact, her pot is heavy, and even though I tried to use it for parties at work, I found it is just easier to bring along a small electric pot that heats up quickly, folds up into a small space, and can be easily stored out of the way in a corner of our equipment room.

But oh, how I love this pot. I love having it so close to me, so close to my writing area. It is better than jewelry, better than a picture, better than just a memory. Just this simple pot brings back my mother and father and Elsie's Shrimp Tempura and John's Dunk Sauce. Shrimp. Sweetie Pie. Love.

Elsie's Shrimp Tempura with John's Dunk Sauce
The Recipes

This recipe seems timeless. As I said, this is the only starter we ever served at Blueberry Hill. My mother must have dipped thousands and thousands of shrimp in batter and hot oil. Now, a number of years later, I find myself doing the same. Whenever we serve these at a party (and we do serve other things, too) guests invariably come right into the kitchen, wanting to snag the puffs before they even get put on a serving tray.

In my catering company, we cook our shrimp in a Fry Daddy (we used to use a Fry Baby, but we outgrew it). This little portable deep fryer, made by the Presto company, is a whole lot easier to haul around than that cast-iron fryer, for one thing, and more important, the electric ones heat up and cool down quickly. Either one will work just fine. I have not noticed any difference in the final product.

Okay—here you go:

Serves 15 or so

The ingredients:

1 quart peanut oil
1 cup all-purpose flour
1 teaspoon table salt
1 teaspoon baking powder
1 cup milk
2 large eggs, lightly beaten with a fork

2 pounds cleaned shrimp (peeled and deveined; make sure to leave the tails on) I like to use "31-35," a medium-size shrimp. Big ones don't cook as well and the small ones are, well, not really worth the effort.

Here's what you do: Heat the oil. If you use an electric cooker, it will only take 3 to 5 minutes. If you use a cast-iron pot, it will take longer. The way to know if the oil is hot enough is to drop a "strike anywhere" match in the oil when you turn the heat on. (These are also known as kitchen matches, but make sure you have the kind with the little white tip; the regular ones will not light on their own.) When the oil is hot enough, the match will ignite, and you're ready to go!

To make the batter, mix the flour, salt, and baking powder in a medium mixing bowl. Add the milk and eggs. Mix, using a fork, until the batter is just barely blended. Do not overwork. Do not try to get rid of every single tiny lump.

Once the oil is hot, take the shrimp, one at a time, dip them in the batter (holding on to the tail) and then lower into the oil. The shrimp will immediately start bubbling and cooking. Keep an eye on the pot. After about 1 minute the shrimp will float to the surface. Coax the half-cooked shrimp to turn over, and cook the other side for another minute or so, just until the batter is a light gold. (In my Fry Daddy I can cook four or five shrimp at a time. Put them in one after another, so they cook at almost the same time.) Remove from the oil with a slotted spoon, drain on paper towels, and serve with John's Dunk Sauce.

John's Dunk Sauce

Makes 2 cups

The ingredients:

1 tablespoon red wine vinegar

2 tablespoons fresh lemon juice

2 tablespoons grated horseradish

1/2 cup ketchup

1 tablespoon Worcestershire sauce

1 tablespoon grated onion

1 1/4 cups mayonnaise (I only use Hellmann's)

1/2 teaspoon table salt

Here's what you do: Mix all the ingredients in a small bowl. Cover and keep in the fridge until you need it.

Serve the Dunk Sauce in a small bowl on a platter with the shrimp and a second small bowl for shrimp tails. Yum!

Note: If you don't use all the Dunk Sauce, stick the leftover in the fridge and use it as a dip with fresh vegetables, as a spread on a sandwich, or slathered on an omelet. It's quite versatile and will last for a good week or so, if you don't eat it all first.

Chapter Three

Sugar Pops

 I grew up eating Sugar Pops for dinner.

Sugar Pops? How is it possible that the daughter of Elsie Masterton grew up eating breakfast cereal instead of Shrimp Steamed in Beer, or Blueberry Hill Cod Baked with Sour Cream and Green Peppers, or Leg of Lamb with Coffee and Mustard Glaze? The truth is: I did not like any of those things. I guess, looking back at myself, I can say I was a picky eater.

My parents' rule stated that my sisters and I had to eat at least one bite of a new item at every single meal and had to really taste it. The hope was, of course, that we would like it, would open our taste buds to new flavors. But after that bite, if we didn't like the food, we could have cereal for dinner.

I ate a lot of cereal.

My mother bought those little boxes of cereal for our guests. Now, most guests were delighted to have my mother's breakfast special of the day: pancakes, waffles, omelets, those kinds of things. But she had to have those little cereals around just in case some guest came along wanting Raisin Bran or Special K or Corn Flakes. Occasionally, a guest chose a box of Sugar Frosted Flakes, but no adult ever touched the Sugar Smacks and Sugar Pops. Those, I was always delighted to find, were generally left—for me.

I suppose we all remember sitting at the dinner table staring at a plate of something that just seemed too horrible to consider eating. I know I did. Peas were off my list. So was fish. I didn't like lamb, and I did not eat green peppers. As a baby, I put Jell-O on my head, though I imagine that was because it amused my sisters so much the first time I did it that I kept it up, just to be cute. One evening when I was five or so, I "doctored" my macaroni so much that it was barely visible underneath all my additions: ketchup, soy sauce, Worcestershire sauce, salt, and a *lot* of pepper. My father watched me shake and garnish and add to the growing plate of inedibility.

"Don't play with your food," he scolded, as I poked and pushed the conglomeration around my plate, hoping to be excused from the table. That evening I had no such luck.

"You're going to have to eat that, young lady," he continued.

Encouraged by my sisters' glances and hidden smiles, I kept going, shaking on a second round of ketchup and then adding pepper until the macaroni was nearly black.

"I mean it," my father growled, "you're going to sit there until midnight. You'll sit there until you clean that plate." At ten that night, after my mother's pleadings finally overcame my father's scolding, he sent me to bed.

After that the rules changed. I guess my parents didn't like sitting there any more than I did. From then on, if we really did try our food and we really did not like it, we could substitute cereal. I was delighted! I *loved* cereal!

I especially loved those little boxes that, if carefully cut, became a cereal bowl, the tops scored in the shape of an H, cut and flipped open like doors into a sweet world. I always spilled milk outside of the waxed paper liner, and sometimes cut through the bottom of the box so the milk poured out onto the table, but at least I ate with the rest of my family and got to be a part of our dinner conversations. That, I guess, was better than not eating at all.

Cereal continues to be my comfort food. After catering a party, if I get home late and have not eaten dinner, I pour a bowl of cereal and sit in front of the television and decompress, letting the guests and the details of the party slip away. I have replaced my childhood bowls of sugar with more grown-up choices like Grape Nuts or Alpen or Cheerios or even one of those health food store choices—you know, the ones that say things to make us think they are good for us. And who knows, they might be, though they usually remind me of a bowl full of sawdust, to tell the truth.

But I must say, I am always happy to be visiting somewhere and find that all the grown-up cereals have been taken and the only remaining options are those little boxes of kid cereals. And I'm happiest of all when there is one little box of Sugar Pops. That's the one I choose.

Chapter Four

Peanut Butter and Marshmallow Fluff

 Miss Moore taught me about Peanut Butter and Marshmallow Fluff. Delores White and I ate a lot of Peanut Butter and Marshmallow Fluff Sandwiches with Miss Moore. We always said the entire name of the sandwich, so I continue to do so now. (In my mind, even then, the importance of the parts and the name of the sandwich were so special that, really, the whole name—all the parts—deserves not to be only written in big letters but really should be surrounded by flashing lights.) I remember eating *only* Peanut Butter and Marshmallow Fluff Sandwiches when I was with Miss Moore, but the adult in me knows she must had given me other foods, too. If I called her now, she'd probably list a whole menu of things she cooked for me, but the thing that sticks with me is this.

I spent a lot of time with Miss Moore and her parents, Mrs. Moore and Mr. Moore. Miss Moore made dolls and sold them from a table in the front room of the Moore house, which was right across the street from the Forest Dale Elementary School, about five miles from Blueberry Hill. In addition to selling dolls, Miss Moore also took care of children. For quite a long time Delores White and I were the only children at Miss Moore's. Delores White's mother brought Delores to Miss Moore's every morning. Delores, still sleeping and still in her pajamas, didn't wake up until her mother had been at work for a few hours. My mother dropped me off whenever she went away on a trip to visit her editor in New York or whenever she and my father needed to travel for business. By the time I reached third grade, my mother had published four books. In those days, that meant a lot of trips to visit one's editor.

I stayed with the Moores a lot.

Delores White and I had a regular routine. We played in the lovely dark space underneath Miss Moore's selling table, me taking huge stitches to hold the seams of my doll dresses together. Delores made small stitches and her doll clothes stayed together much longer than mine did, but I was much faster. My goal was to sew as fast as possible so I could get out to the shed with Mr. Moore and help him skin squirrels or feed the ducks or water the garden. Delores White liked sewing. I did not.

We also helped Mrs. Moore, Mr. Moore, and Miss Moore with the laundry. The Moores had an old washing machine that hooked up to their sink. Wash day happened when the sun shone. Mr. Moore pushed the fat white enameled machine into the kitchen, plugged it into the wall outlet and filled the tank with water. The house shook as the machine swished the tub full of clothes around and back, around and back. When the wash cycles finished, Miss Moore fed each piece of clothing through rollers above the machine, squeezing the water out of the clothes like toothpaste. Miss Moore warned us to keep back. A little girl's arm could get trapped and dragged in and broken. She'd seen it happen! After all the water was cranked out, Mr. Moore and Delores White and I hung everything on the line out back.

But days at Miss Moore's revolved around lunch. And lunch each day, as I recall, was exactly the same: a Peanut Butter and Marshmallow Fluff Sandwich (crusts on, cut into four squares—*not* triangles!), Potato Chips, and Chicken Noodle Soup. Then Miss Moore gave us one nickel to take to the Red and White store on the corner where we agonized over Popsicles and which flavor to buy: orange or purple or red. The clerk at the checkout took our nickel and split the Popsicle for us. We skipped back to Miss Moore's, just in time for a nap.

Delores White and I memorized the Marshmallow Fluff song and sang it all the time.

Oh you need Fluff Fluff Fluff to make a Fluffernutter
Marshmallow Fluff and lots of peanut butter.
First you spread spread spread
Your bread with peanut butter
And Marshmallow Fluff and that's a Fluffernutter.
When you enjoy joy joy
Your Fluff and peanut butter
Make sure you have enough for another Fluffernutter.

Delores White and I did not call our sandwiches Fluffernutters, but we did always say the whole name, slurring it together a bit: Peanut ButternMarshmallow Fluff.

The other day, shopping for my groceries near here, I saw a jar of Marshmallow Fluff on one of the lower shelves, near the peanut butter. Amazing, I observed: it had not changed one bit, but was still a bumpy, fat jar with a blue lid, the blue letters on the label showing up clearly against the snow white "fluff" inside, the type unchanged. I toyed with the idea of buying and tasting some for the memory of it all. I opted not to.

Some things are best left to memory.

Marshmallow Fluff and Fluffernutter are registered trademarks of Durkee-Mower, Inc. and the Fluffernutter song is copyrighted material owned by Durkee-Mower, Inc., and all are used with express permission of Don Durkee.

Chapter Five

Dinner at The Big House

"Come on, Laurey," Janie called from the porch of the schoolhouse, "it's time for you to get dressed. It's your night at The Big House!"

My night at The Big House! Finally! Lucinda had her first turn when she was seven. Heather, too. Now it was my turn: my first night for dinner in the dining room of Blueberry Hill. I jumped off the swing set and skipped inside. Heather kept on swinging, acting like she didn't care. But I did! It was finally my turn.

Fred Lord had invited me. A formal invitation, it was. "Laurey," he'd said the day before, "your mother tells me you are now old enough to come to the dining room and have dinner with the adults. I'd like to have the pleasure of your company tomorrow evening if you could find a space for me on your dance card." Fred was a regular at the Inn. He came every year, stayed for a week or two, and was so much a part of our world that we named his room after him: Fred's Room.

I grinned. My mother had reminded me, back in May, that now that I was seven I was old enough to be invited to sit with the guests at the Inn. Normally in the summer time, when we had the most guests, my sisters and I ate with Janie, our "governess," down the road in the old schoolhouse that we called The Cottage. It was just a little house. Not like the Inn, which was a very big house. We lived at the Inn in the winters when we didn't have very many guests, but in the summers the three of us moved to be out of the way.

We drove to Lake Dunmore with Janie every day in the summer and spent the whole day there. I would have liked it better if I could have just stayed home, because my favorite place in the whole world was the kitchen of the Inn, but all the grownups thought I was too young to be there, so most of the time I went with Lucinda and Heather to the lake. In the fall, when we had fewer guests, my sisters and I shared the bedroom right above the kitchen, a warm room under the eaves that filled with delicious morning kitchen smells, bacon and toast and coffee and maple syrup, at breakfast. At night we lay in bed, listening to the guests walking through the kitchen as they left the dining room on the way back to their rooms.

"Dinner was delicious, Elsie," they'd say. "The best meal I've ever had in my whole life."

"You've outdone yourself this time, Elsie. I've been here a month and you have not repeated yourself yet. You're amazing!"

"Wow! You just keep getting better and better!"

"Come on, Laurey!" It was Janie again, scrubbing the dirt off my knees. "You really need to help me if you are going to get dressed in time!"

She helped me take off my shorts and pull on a clean white blouse. "Here," she said, "this Swedish jumper will be cute."

I squirmed into it. I wished I could have just kept my shorts on, but Janie insisted on the dress. It wasn't that bad, really. One of the guests, whom we called Aunt Jampy even though she was not our real aunt, traveled around the world, sending back three outfits from wherever she went. The Swedish outfits weren't bad. I really liked the kilts from Scotland, but it was too hot in the summer to wear them. And the headdresses she'd sent from Africa were fun to look at but not much fun to wear since the sharp points poked into my head. Sweden it would be for My First Night in the Dining Room.

Janie walked me up the hill to the Inn. I bounced alongside her with excitement.

My father greeted us at the front door. "Good evening, young lady," he said, his eyes twinkling. "Come right in. Your dining companion is awaiting your arrival." I smiled up at him. He winked. "Now you pay attention to Fred," he reminded me. "This is a big night for you."

I skipped into the den. Fred sat on the couch, talking to other guests and waiting for me. He looked so nice, grey pants and blue blazer. I had grey pants and a blue blazer too, but, well, Janie had said I needed to wear a skirt tonight. When Fred saw me he stood up and was so tall his head almost reached the tip of Daddy's swordfish mounted on the wall behind him. My sisters and I spent winter afternoons in the den, reading in front of the fireplace, staring up at that fish, caught by our father when he and my mother were in Florida. Fred could easily look that fish right in the eye. Boy, was he tall!

"How ah you?" he boomed in his Boston accent. "What a pleasure it is to have you for a dining companion this evening."

"I'm very well, thank you. And thank you very much for inviting me," I said, practicing using these new words.

I looked over at my father who watched, beaming at me.

Fred kept up a constant conversation. I mostly listened, nodded, snuck glances at my father who'd nod and smile, letting me know I was doing the right thing. When Lucinda came in and offered Shrimp Tempura with John's Dunk Sauce I waited until everyone else had been served and then carefully picked one up by the tail, dunked it in the sauce, and put it in my own monkey dish before eating it. I wiped my mouth with my napkin. I was doing just what the other grownups were doing. Lucinda was eleven and knew how to do everything! She even got to work. Eating at The Big House was one thing, but more than that I couldn't wait until I was old enough to work there, just like Lucinda.

When we all had been served two shrimp each, all of the guests, me included, were escorted through the kitchen into the dining room. I followed Fred, and just as we were about to turn past the refrigerator into the dining room, I caught my mother's eye. She smiled, too, watching me follow Fred and then, turning, opened the oven and popped in a tray filled with her tiny biscuits. She winked at me, knowing how much I loved them. In the winter I got to help her make them. Tonight, though, I was a guest! And soon I would get to eat them, hot out of the oven like everyone else. What a night!

Franklin and Caroline Pillsbury were already seated at a small, square table in the corner of the dining room just on the other side of the white birch tree that held up the middle of the dining room ceiling. Franklin stood up as we neared the table, and pulled out my chair. "Here you go, young lady," his voice, rich and smooth, comforted me. Last week Heather had been their guest and the week before it had been Lucinda's turn. The Pillsburys stayed for a month each summer, Franklin roaming around taking photographs of the land, of the Inn, of all of us.

"Shall we?" invited Fred, picking up his fork. "Here's to you!" he gestured to me.

I did exactly what he did, picking up my fork, gesturing back to him, and then cutting off a small piece of my cantaloupe. Fred cut off a little bit of ham and ate it with his melon. I did too. Fred smiled at me. I smiled at him. This was fun!

Connie, one of the college girls who helped in the dining room came and cleared our empty plates. As she left the dining room, Lani, the college girl from Hawaii, came in, carrying our huge wooden salad bowl filled with a Blueberry Hill Tossed Salad. Lani circled the dining room, coming to our table at the end. I, as tradition dictated, was last to be served. I took the wooden spoon and fork in one hand and, doing just as I had watched my father do, served myself, taking the lettuce, the cucumbers, the blue cheese, the rings of Bermuda onions, and a couple of capers. I tried to avoid the anchovies.

As we ate our salads, Connie returned with a basket filled with Elsie's bite-sized biscuits, steaming under their napkin. I took three. Hot biscuits! Yum-mee! Fred watched as I took three little cubes of butter and tucked a whole cube into each biscuit. I took my first biscuit, spooned on some blueberry jam, and popped it into my mouth. It was only after I had started chewing this mouthful of hot, buttery, sweet biscuit, that I noticed Fred carefully cutting his butter into thin slivers before putting a small piece on his biscuit and spooning a little bit of jam from his bread and butter plate. Oops! On my second one I did just what he had done, which made him and the Pillsburys smile again.

After our salads were cleared, the dining room grew quiet as my father wheeled in the rolling buffet table. Tonight's dinner was Roast Beef. My father went around the dining room asking each guest about their preferences. I watched him sharpen his knife and saw him cut off the end piece, tucking it off to one side as he sliced rare and medium rare pieces for most of the guests. When it came time for our table he served Fred, and then, finally, me! He put that hidden end piece of Roast Beef on a plate, added some Noodles with Sherry and a spoonful of Baby Carrots with Fresh Dill.

"Here you go, PQ," he said, calling me by my pet name. Loretta Mason Potts was an odd character in one of our bedtime stories, a feisty girl who never quite fit in—until her brother and sister discovered she was really a queen in a secret world. He called me Loretta sometimes, and sometimes "Loretta P-for-Potts," which then got shortened to "Loretta P" and then lengthened to "Loretta P-which-goes-with-Q" and finally, short again, to just "PQ." I must be doing okay, I thought—he called me PQ in front of all these people *and* he gave me the end piece.

I continued to do what Fred did, eating small bites of my dinner and remembering about not talking with my mouth full. I said thank you when Fred passed something and please if I needed more. I wiped my mouth on my napkin when I was finished. Whew—dinner at The Big House took a long time!

And then came dessert. By this time I was getting very sleepy, but managed to stay awake for a small piece of something. My mother served our table last, of course. I was at the very end. I did not want Fruit Compote in Wine and I did not care for any Coffee Cream Torte. I politely said no thank you to Apple Nut "Thing," and declined a piece of Blueberry Apple Crisp, too. I did, ultimately, say yes to a small piece of Mama's Sponge Cake with Sour Cream Sauce and Hot Blueberries, and then, as Connie was beginning to come around the dining room with coffee I asked, politely, if I could please be excused. Fred stood up as I left the dining room. I walked into the kitchen, hugged my mother good night, and took my father's hand as he walked me down the road back to the cottage where Janie helped me put on my pajamas, brush my teeth, say my prayers, and climb into bed. I was asleep before she finished singing the lullaby that night.

Chapter Six

Pink Sno-Balls

 In first grade, everyone seemed to have better lunches than the ones my mother packed for me. And at the Forest Dale Elementary School there was no cafeteria, so what we ate was just what our mothers had packed. It never occurred to me that the food my sisters and I ate at home was any different than anyone else's until I started school. And though I gradually became aware that other kids brought different foods, the first big explosion of my culinary education happened the day I left my lunch at home.

"Okay, children," Miss Jones said, after this discovery had been made. "Laurey forgot her lunch, so would each one of you please give her a little bit of yours? I'm sure she'll do the same for you if you forget to bring your lunch one day."

Everyone opened up paper bags, lunch pails, lunch boxes. Scott Johnson had tuna fish on white bread and gave me a half. I'd eaten tuna fish before but his tasted very different, with little bits of sweet relish in it and lots of mayonnaise, too. And I was sure I'd never eaten that kind of bread, invitingly white, squishy, and very soft. I made a mental note to tell my mother about it, sure the guests at Blueberry Hill would love it too.

"You never ate Sunbeam bread?" Scott asked, incredulous, when I exclaimed about it. "What *do* you eat at your house?"

"Pepperidge Farms," I murmured, embarrassed. I would definitely have to tell my mother about this. And furthermore, Scott's sandwich was cut in halves. He had given me a whole rectangle. *My* sandwiches were always cut into triangles. Rectangles tasted *much* better than triangles, I was realizing. And look how much time you saved by only having *two* sandwiches instead of *four*! I couldn't wait to tell my mother.

Debbie Brown had barbecued potato chips. *Wow!* She gave me a whole little bag of my own.

"You mean you never ate barbecued potato chips?" she blurted out with laughter as she watched me open and taste the salty delights. "How about French fries? *No!?* Corn chips?" I sat and shook my head, burning with embarrassment.

The lunch feast continued: Julie LaFrance gave me part of a "baloney" sandwich with a tidy square of American cheese! Delores White's gift was a silky smooth Skippy peanut butter and grape jelly sandwich! Before that I'd only ever had my mother's Blueberry Jam. Grape jelly was great! I ate with considerable pleasure, trying to remember all of these amazing foods. My mother, I knew, was writing a new cookbook while my sisters and I were at school. Surely she'd want to include these things.

"Okay, children," Miss Jones's voice interrupted my daydreaming. "Does anyone have any dessert they'd like to share with Laurey?"

My desk became a buffet: one Oreo cookie, a Hostess Twinkie, and a couple of chocolate-covered graham crackers piled up in an exquisite stack. Other children donated candy. Finally, when I couldn't in my wildest imagination conceive of anything more splendid, Reginald Carey shuffled over.

"I have two Sno-balls," he said sadly, adding to my stack. "Here's one for you."

"That's very nice of you, Reginald," Miss Jones said. "You're a very generous boy."

I stared at Reginald's gift. It was utterly mesmerizing, a soft pink mound, covered with flakes of white coconut. It quivered on my desk. I picked it up, brought it to my mouth. The whole thing was a mass of soft marshmallow, it turned out, and it fit in my hand perfectly. I turned it over. It was soft inside, too, with damp pink cake and bright red jelly, more coconut and even some creamy pink filling. I could not imagine anything finer, and stowed it at the edge of my smorgasbord, saving it for last.

That afternoon, when my sisters and I piled into my mother's car, I exploded with my new discoveries. "Scott's mother cuts his sandwiches in half! And he had soft white bread. Why don't WE have soft white bread?"

"Library paste bread!" hooted Lucinda, four years older and ever so much smarter. "That bread is horrible!"

"But I liked it!" I protested. "It wasn't all crumbly like that stuff we have. And can you please cut my sandwiches into halves and not those little triangles? No one else has triangles! And can we get some pink Sno-balls? Please?"

But no matter how hard I lobbied, my lunches did not change very much. I was not able to talk anyone into buying the plastic-bagged white bread. My cookies continued to be homemade (which, I eventually realized, were much better—though you could not convince me of that at age seven.) And my mother refused to buy any pink Sno-balls.

For the most part, I remembered to bring my lunch for the rest of the year, but I never felt bad when, hopping out of the car to go into school, I realized that my brown paper bag was probably still on the counter back home in the kitchen of the Inn. It was probably filled with a Cream Cheese and Olive Sandwich, a little bag full of Carrot Sticks and a couple of Black Olives, an Old-Fashioned Dark Molasses Cookie, and, perhaps, a Golden Apple from the tree outside the dining room.

I couldn't wait for lunch!

Chapter Seven

Sour Cream Waffles

 I woke up this morning thinking about breakfast, which is not such a big surprise, I guess, since it is morning, after all. Here I am at work, having just eaten a raisin-filled sticky bun. Every once in a while, though not this morning, I get a breakfast-cooking urge and come to work early to fire up our griddle and make breakfast for the gang here: blueberry pancakes, sausages, bacon (baked with a drizzle of Vermont Maple Syrup), and coffee. These work breakfasts always remind me of one specific breakfast at Blueberry Hill.

My sisters and I shared the bedroom right above the kitchen at the Inn. The stairway just up the landing to one of the eight doors leading to our kitchen, led up to Our Room. Called Our Room even when we moved to another house and turned that room into one for guests, it could be a sweetly aromatic place, especially in the mornings when we woke to the smell of bacon and coffee drifting up the tiny staircase.

Guests at the Inn wandered down from their rooms, through the kitchen and into the dining room for breakfast. My mother, standing at her stove making pancakes or eggs or omelets, greeted them, offered coffee, and mentioned her special for the morning. Each day there was one special because Blueberry Hill was not a short order joint. Breakfast was no snap meal there, but was an event, meant to be lingered over, savored, appreciated.

That morning—the one I remember so well—my mother had planned Sour Cream Waffles. And oh, what waffles! The batter, mixed at the beginning the same way most batters are, becomes extra special when blended with sour cream and then folded into beaten egg whites. The result is a lovely, light waffle. Light, that is, but rich and decadent in its own way. (I still make these, but only for very special occasions, you know, fat and calories and such being the health considerations they are these days.) The batter does not keep well, since the egg whites fall after an hour or so. If you mix up a batch of the batter, you'd better know you're going to make that many waffles. That day my mother had made a double batch of batter in anticipation of the day's special. She'd winked at me, knowing they were my favorite. I'd get one after the guests were done.

"This morning I am making our delicious Sour Cream Waffles," she said to the first guest, "though if you prefer, I'll be happy to make you something else." The guest didn't even stop and think before blurting out, "I would *love* to have a Poached Egg, Elsie! Been thinking about one all night for some reason."

Graciously, my mother put a saucepan of water on the stove, added a splash of white vinegar, brought it to a boil, twirled the water into a whirlpool with the handle of a wooden spoon, and poached his egg into a wispy swirl. She put it on a toasted English muffin and let me carry it into the dining room.

When the next guest arrived, my mother repeated the special, along with her offer to make something different, which that guest accepted! "Oh, a scrambled egg, please, Elsie, and please make it dry. And I'd love some dry toast, please." My mother, polite, cooked. The egg. Not a waffle.

The third guest, unbelievably, did not want waffles, either. "You know, pancakes are what I have been reading about. And pancakes are what I have been dreaming about. So could you, would you, agree to make me some Blueberry Pancakes, Elsie?" She sighed, agreed.

Similarly, the fourth guest wanted a different breakfast, as did the fifth, sixth, seventh, and eighth. Fifteen guests and not one guest would have a waffle. Nor did anyone ask for another guest's choice.

"An omelet would be delicious, Elsie."

"Just French toast today for me, thanks, Elsie."

"Corned beef hash with a sunny side-up egg would be great, Elsie."

She cooked it all, just like a short-order cook, except with a visibly rising exasperation. Her nostrils flared, her eyebrows lowered. She started to bite the corner of her lip; her mouth, agitated, expressed her displeasure.

Breakfast at Blueberry Hill was served between eight and nine. Now, this was not a hard and fast rule, but generally guests knew that if they wanted breakfast (and who wouldn't?) those were the hours of service. Sure, a guest could come down early, get a cup of coffee and sit and talk with my mother while she cooked. But he would get served his breakfast at eight. And a latecomer would get breakfast, but could quickly see that it would have been better if he had gotten to the dining room on time. No one was late twice.

That morning, around nine thirty, well after everything was cleaned and put away, well after I had finished my waffle, and well after the griddle had cooled down, one final guest arrived.

He was late.

Very late.

My mother looked up in amazement at this final straw of her morning.

"Good morning," she said, trying to be courteous, sweeping the last crumb from the counter. "Today we have, as our special breakfast, Sour Cream Waffles, though I'd be happy to make something different for you if you prefer."

Her eyes tightened, her words came out like chips of ice.

The guest could see and hear that something was wrong. He understood, in that instant, that he was late. He immediately realized his inconvenience. He saw she would have to take all the ingredients back out of the refrigerator, heat up the griddle, and start, as it were, from scratch.

"Oh Elsie," he said, smiling, trying to be helpful, "I'll just have what everyone else had."

My mother did not need a second invitation. She waved him into the dining room. "It'll be just a few minutes."

But then she started to sparkle! It would be possible, after all, to find something humorous in that morning's ordeal. I tucked myself into a chair and watched.

She did, indeed, make what everyone else had eaten. All of it. In a flash she made one poached egg, one scrambled egg, one blueberry pancake, and one piece of French toast. She made one portion of oatmeal and one serving of corned beef hash with a sunnyside-up egg. She got out one little box of Raisin Bran, whipped up one portion of Cream of Wheat, and sizzled one piece of bacon and one piece of sausage. She made one omelet, warmed one blueberry muffin. Finally she toasted one piece of toast. Dry. She heaped it all on one platter and topped it with one perfect, fluffy Sour Cream Waffle.

She gave it to me to carry into the dining room, this platter, this personal buffet. And my mother, that one time, came with me.

"Here you go," she said, as I put the plate in front of the guest, "just what everyone else ordered!"

The guest stared at his plate, looked at my mother, and burst out laughing. The other guests, lingering over their coffee, looked up, and then they too broke into laughter, all at once realizing what all their orders had meant for my mother, the sole cook. They rose and gave her a standing ovation, joining her in the morning's joke and thanking her, in the best way they knew, for their special breakfasts.

And to his credit, the guest of honor ate his entire breakfast. Every single bite of it.

Elsie's Sour Cream Waffles
The Recipe

These are still amazing. Because they are rich, I only make them for special occasions now—but any old day can easily become a "Special Occasion" with the right slant, right?

Here's my mother's recipe.

Makes 8 to 10 small waffles.

The ingredients:
 1 cup sifted flour (my mother used cake flour; I use whatever I have)
 1 teaspoon baking powder $\frac{1}{2}$ tablespoon sugar
 1 teaspoon baking soda   3 large eggs
 $\frac{1}{8}$ teaspoon salt   1 pint sour cream

Here's what you do: Get the waffle iron heating.

Mix the batter: Sift all the dry ingredients together. Separate the eggs. Beat the egg yolks thoroughly and then add the sour cream. Mix this into the sifted dry ingredients. Do it quickly and don't try to get every tiny bit smooth. Just mix 'em and be done with it.

Whip the egg whites until peaks form. Don't mix so long that they dry out, but do look for those soft peaks.

Fold the egg whites into the flour-egg mixture. Again, don't over mix.

Following the specifics of your waffle iron, make the waffles. The most important thing here is to stop cooking before the waffles are completely cooked. They are much better if slightly undercooked. There is no harm here with uncooked food—the waffles will continue to cook a bit after you take them off the iron—but they'll be so much better than they would if you waited until they were completely cooked all the way through before removing them. Trust me on this one!

I always serve my mother's waffles with hot Vermont Maple Syrup and salted butter. Usually when I cook I use unsalted butter so I can control the flavor of the food. With waffles, I prefer the salted kind—it tastes perfect to me, combined with the sweetness of the syrup. I prefer

Grade B or even C Maple Syrup. I like the more intense flavor of the syrup made later in the season. Dark. Rich. Wonderful.

Note: My mother says that this recipe makes enough for about 8 to 10 small waffles. But I made them for my sisters and some friends at Christmas last year and, though we started with plates and civility, by the time I reached the bottom of the bowl of batter, we were eating them with our hands right off the serving platter. The six of us were completely stuffed. And very, very happy, I might add.

Chapter Eight

"Kleenex. Chapstick. Dime to Call Home."

 If I have them all I must be ready to go. If I don't, I most certainly am not.

I start most days, especially when the weather gets cold, thinking of my father. We lived eight miles from school, beyond the reach of the town school bus. My father, the designated chauffeur, drove us into town each morning. With three girls, he found himself turning around to go home for some forgotten thing far too often. He, of course, never forgot anything, but he'd had much more time to practice, I suppose.

As I sit here with a drippy nose from a cold, I think of one particular drive. Lucinda, Heather, and I, tucked into the back seat of the car, sniffed. One of us, I'm sure, always sniffed. One of us, I'm sure, usually had hay fever or a cold. The sniffer tried to hide, but inevitably our father honed in.

"Who is sniffing?" he barked. "And where is your handkerchief? I bought you girls handkerchiefs, didn't I? Where is your handkerchief?"

"I forgot it, Daddy," came the hushed reply.

Huffing, he'd lean onto his left hip, reach around, pull *his* handkerchief from his right hip pocket, fold it, and, impatient, hand it to the unfortunate sniffing girl who would dab the drip and quickly hand the handkerchief back.

Unfortunate, too, was the daughter who, sitting next to him in the front seat on the way home from skiing, made the mistake of licking chapped lips.

"Where is your Chapstick?" he'd scold. "Didn't I give each of you girls your own Chapstick? How is it that you never have Chapstick? For crying out loud!" He'd reach into his jacket, pull out *his* Chapstick, uncap it, twist the bottom until the lipstick was perfectly extended, and hand it to the front seat daughter. "For crying out loud! You'd lose your head if it wasn't attached!"

The daughter hastily but gratefully coated her lips and quietly handed the tube back.

In time, his routine became a family joke. With three of us, someone always forgot something. And after a while Daddy sang out the list before we even left the house. "Kleenex" started us off. "Handkerchief" was outmoded and replaced once those little packets of Kleenex appeared at Brown's Pharmacy. "Chapstick" came next. "Homework," forgotten a couple of times, got added to the list. In the winter "hat" and "mittens" drew top billing even when my sisters, older and fashion conscious, deliberately left theirs at home.

My father's list always ended with "and a dime to call home." Now, there were no pay phones in Goshen or Forest Dale or Brandon, but "and a dime to call home" closed out the routine. Somewhere, we understood, they *did* have pay phones and so *those* people would have to remember this essential item. It wouldn't hurt to be prepared, because we might go there sometime.

And, I might add, we liked being in on the joke.

Even now, on most mornings, I still find myself going through the list that is now mine, my father's voice ringing clearly in my mind: "Kleenex, Chapstick, lunch money, homework, and a dime to call home."

And most mornings, I find, I have *almost* everything on the list.

Chapter Nine

Haying

August was haying time in Vermont. Around here, in the mountains of North Carolina, people cut their first load of hay in June or even in late May sometimes, which has always seemed odd to me because at home when I was growing up, it took all the way until the middle of August for the grass in the fields around Blueberry Hill to be long enough to cut. I guess it happens earlier here with warmer temperatures and all. Maybe it happened earlier then, but August is the time I remember. An internal reminder still clicks on for me toward the end of the summer. Time to cut the hay. Time to fill the barn.

It was so quiet on our road that I started hearing Bob Wanser's tractor chugging when he was still way down by the Carter house. From my perch in my maple tree, the big one right across the road from the Inn, the noise coming closer and closer meant that Bob was on his way. As the tractor came over the hill by The Red Barn, I could see that he had his cutting blade attached, hitched up at an angle to keep from catching every branch on the side of the road.

"Bob!" I scrambled down from the tree.

"Look out," he yelled back. "Watch out for that blade, you'll get hoit!"

Bob said "hoit" because he was, he told us, from Brooklyn. He said, "troilah" for trailer and "beeah" for beer. We laughed at his speech, tried to imitate him, and found we couldn't. But that didn't matter. It was haying time!

"Can I come with you when you go get the hay trailer?" I hollered over the noise of the engine. "Can I?"

"Go tell ya muthuh," he grumbled, though I knew he didn't mean it, the grumbling that is. Bob was always happy to have me along.

And so began three days of driving back and forth over the roads from Blueberry Hill to the Wansers way over on the other side of Goshen, past Goshen Four Corners, past the Asensio's, past Baker's Acre, past the Crippled Children's Camp. Back and forth we went, Bob sitting me on the front of the tractor seat, letting me steer, and only occasionally yelling at me. "Watch where ya goin!" he'd say if we came too close to the edge of the road. "Let me take ovah," he'd say when he sensed I was getting scared right before the hill that dipped way down and then way back up right before Baker's Acre. "You can steer once we get up to the top."

We needed to get the rake and the trailer before we could do anything else, which was just fine with me, because then I got to drive more. Mark Hayes, who was exactly my age, drove his father's tractor all by himself, but Bob said that nine was too young for that so I had to sit and be happy with just steering. And then, right after Bob said that, Mark fell off the trailer and broke his arm and that meant Bob was right, just like he told us he was.

When Bob finally had all his machines at our house, after all the trips back and forth to his farm, he cut our hay, driving around and around our field. "You stay away," he instructed, "You could get hoit. This rake ain't no place for youse kids."

I had a grand view from my maple tree and I watched as the hay fell away from his blade. Bob knew where all our rocks were and avoided them cleanly on his passes around the field. By the time the last of the grass was cut, Bob knew he could start to rake. Warning me to keep my distance, he switched the cutting blade for the rake and drove around the field again, the tines of the rotating fork catching the cut grass and sweeping it into a long snaking pile. Around and around and around. It was like the rake was a giant hand, the fingers guiding the grass. My fingers twitched as I imagined them raking.

"Pfewf, it's hot!" he sputtered. "Go grab me a beeah outta that coolah. And watch that tab—you don't want to get hoit." Bob showed me how to take the tab off the top of the beer can and put it back inside the can (the tabs came completely off in those days). "You would-n't want caows to eat it, it'd rip up their stomachs," he explained. I nodded, took off the tab of Bob's beer and tucked it into the can. I looked at Bob expectantly. "Yeah, go ahead. One sip is all. One." I sipped the cold drink and handed the can to him.

"All right," he said after he finished his beer. "See ya damarrah."

The next morning, early, Bob and his wife Muriel chugged over the hill. She sat perched on the front of the bailer, its square hay chamber making a solid seat. She wore blue jeans, a blue bandana tied at her forehead, and a sleeveless white shirt which she knotted up over her flat belly. She was "very stylish," my mother'd said.

Wasting no time, Bob started the slow route around the fields, steering so yesterday's piles of now-dried grass fed right into the open mouth of the baler, which clicked and murmured and ate and ate and ate the hay until, just like that, a tight bale plopped out of the back.

Heather and I tried to count the seconds, the clicks of the machine, to predict when the bales would pop out. Muriel walked along beside and tossed the bales into piles of three or four. Bob drove up and down, bouncing along as the baler spit out its tight rectangles.

Finally it was time to load the "troilah." Muriel drove this time. As she passed the little piles of bales, Bob picked them up and tossed them onto the trailer bed. A couple of volunteers usually helped too. The college boys who worked at Blueberry Hill for the summer welcomed the change of pace from setting the tables or mowing the lawn, and piled the bales as Bob threw. Around and around they went, hauling, tossing, piling, until all the bales were loaded.

And then Bob sent the boys up to the hay loft of our barn, drove the loaded trailer right to the door, and tossed the bales up to the boys' waiting hands. Our bales were smaller than usual so that my sister Lucinda could pick them up. They were plenty heavy for her, but for Bob and the college boys, the tossing was easy. They unloaded half the trailer and left the rest for Bob. Half for Bob, half for us. That was the arrangement.

At the end of that day, after another beer, Bob and Muriel sputtered off down the road, past The Red Barn and up over the hill by the Carters where the sound of the tractor motor faded into the hills. They'd be back for the rest of the machinery tomorrow. And they'd be back to cut our hay again next year. For now our barn was full, the fields were trim, and everything was "jest roit."

Chapter Ten

To Tell The Truth

 "I get to leave school early today!" I crowed to my third grade classmates, waving my note from home. "My mother is going to be on *To Tell The Truth*!"

"You lucky slob," Scott Johnson muttered.

I was particularly fond of that expression, "you lucky slob," and had, as a matter of fact, used it just a few months earlier, when my father had taken me along with Heather and Lucinda to meet the president of the Vermont Life Insurance Company.

"And this," the president had said to our little family group, "is the teak bowl that the people of Indonesia gave to me and my wife when we visited five years ago."

The bowl, which sat prominently on his side desk, was beautiful.

"You lucky slob!" I'd gushed.

Mr. Vermont Life President turned red, stopped talking, looked at me, coughed, glanced at my father, and then stepped on to the next item on our tour. My father and sisters glared at me, which I did not understand, since I'd paid him my highest compliment. Lucinda waved at me to keep quiet from then on, though I did not know why. Later, when we piled back into the Citroën, my whole family ganged up on me.

"I felt like I wanted to crawl into a hole in the floor!" Lucinda, a sophisticate in seventh grade, had scolded. "Lucky slob! What an insult!"

"Don't you *ever* let me catch you using those words again, young lady," my father barked.

Heather didn't even bother looking at me, unwilling to waste words, though I had, I was sure, heard her use that very same expression in school. Suddenly, her fifth grade self had become too elegant for me and my "childish" expressions.

To me, in third grade, "you lucky slob" was the best we could say about each other, so I could tell Scott was envious, probably mostly because I was getting out of school for the day. Every one of us was in awe of anyone who was actually on TV. Today it was going to be my mother!

My mother, one of the very few mothers in my whole school who worked outside of the home, was already odd. Running an Inn, writing, traveling to New York to promote books, and cooking and having people travel from far away places to stay for weeks at a time was a very different thing for a mother to do, if you compared me to everyone else I knew. At birthday parties in my family we had full meals, with one or two friends invited for the whole evening, everyone sitting down to dinner with my entire family. Other kids in my class had midafternoon angel food cake with pastel-peaked meringue frosting, mother-of-the-birthday-child parties, complete with slices of Neapolitan ice cream (neat stripes of vanilla, chocolate, and strawberry) and those little blow-up whistles that look like a snake unrolling from the blower's mouth. Other kids' mothers proudly made Duncan Hines cakes from a shiny red box. At our house, my mother made her Perfect White Cake, and the birthday child got to choose the color of the butter and confectioner's sugar frosting. The year Heather got a violin as a present, her birthday cake was purple. Mine was deep green one year. But no cake at the Inn ever came out of a box, which was another reason for everyone to think we were odd.

Heather, if the truth be told, was the real lucky slob, since it was her turn to take a trip with Mommy when this television show came along. And instead of just getting to go to New York to see a Broadway musical, stay at the Taft Hotel and eat at Tad's Steak House, Heather was going to get to actually watch the live broadcast of *To Tell The Truth*. Lucinda and I would have to be happy seeing it all on television, which, actually, was fine with me.

"After I come get you we'll pick Lucinda up at Otter Valley," Daddy had said, "and then we'll go to Rutland to watch the show at the Economy Department Store." We didn't have a television set at home, though we'd rent one each year when *The Wizard of Oz* was shown. We'd see Leonard Bernstein's *Young People's Concerts*, too, and *Peter Pan* if the timing was right. But owning a set of our own was out of the question. Everyone we knew had a TV. Everyone but us.

Daddy drove like a race car driver, whipping around curves, taking the back roads to Rutland, past the golf course, flying over the bumps, even getting the car to leave the ground a couple of times. Lucinda and I didn't get carsick, so Daddy sped along. Heather was safe in a studio in New York somewhere so we didn't have to worry about her "Daddy-I'm-going-to-be-sick" peeps from the backseat. He found a parking spot right in front of the department store, turned off the engine of the Citroën, and let the air hiss out of the "hydraulic suspension" that he was so proud of. We hardly noticed as our car lowered to the ground, ignoring the stares from people on the sidewalk. We were used to that, being among the few people in the whole state of Vermont to even own one of the strange French cars. When Lani Morioku, our Hawaiian college student who was one of the Inn's summer waitresses, drove off the road one June, it took months for the replacement part to arrive all the way from France. Our Citroën was an oddity. Another one.

"Let's go, girls." Daddy set a speedy, long-legged pace as he hurried into the store. "Where are the televisions, if you please?" he asked a clerk, and then winked at us as we struggled to keep up. "Hurry, girls, Mommy's going to be on television!"

We arrived at the television area at the exact minute that the *To Tell The Truth* theme music faded and a deep announcer's voice said, "Contestant number one, what is your name please?" and one of three women standing in a silhouette said, "My name is Elsie Masterton."

"Contestant number two, what is your name please?"

A tall, thin silhouette said, "My name is Elsie Masterton."

"And contestant number three, what is *your* name, please?"

The third silhouette, just the right size, said, "My name is Elsie Masterton."

"There she is! There she is! That's Mommy!" I jumped out of my chair. "Look!" I was giddy with excitement.

"I, Elsie Masterton," the announcer said, reading from a script, "along with my husband, John, founded the Blueberry Hill Inn in Goshen, Vermont. Together we built a ski area, but when the snow failed us, we invited guests to come and stay. Ultimately, I wrote about those beginning times, and I have now written three cookbooks and two novels. We have three children: Lucinda, Heather, and Laurey. My name," the announcer finished, "is Elsie Masterton." The lights came up, illuminating each of the three faces. The camera panned to each of them.

"Look! Look! There's Mommy!" I yelled. A few customers heard my commotion and joined our little group.

"Ladies," the host, Bud Collyer, said, "you may be seated."

I could barely contain myself there in the television section of the Economy Department Store in Rutland in the middle of the afternoon on a school day. I hopped out of my chair and ran up to the television screen, waving and squealing. "Hi, Mommy!"

Bud, the host, invited the panelists to question my mother and the two imposters.

"What," Peggy Cass asked, "is a truffle? Contestant number one, please."

"Um, it's a type of spaghetti," stuttered the first one who was not my mother.

"Uh huh. Contestant number two?" Cass said, sneering.

"Actually, it is a kind of fruit," contestant number two said, none too confidently.

"And contestant number three, what do *you* say a truffle is?"

My mother answered about underground fungi that are located with special pigs, being a little too sure of herself. My father whispered to the television set to my mother to remember not to act too smart. Contestants, he reminded the screen, won more money if they fooled the panelists.

"And where, may I ask contestant number two, do capers come from?" asked Orson Bean, prim behind a bow tie.

Contestant number two, even I could see, had no idea what a caper was, so Orson asked my mother. "It is the berry of a nasturtium blossom," my mother answered with confidence. "Sometimes they come from a caper bush, too." Gosh, my mother was smart!

"So why was it so hard to start the Inn?" Kitty Carlisle questioned contestant number one.

Contestant number one was not smooth and fumbled through the answer. The questions continued, the panelists asking the three women food questions. The two imposters didn't really know anything. My mother always answered easily.

Sitting in the Economy we all continued to be very excited. Still more shoppers had gathered around by then, having heard my yelps of delight. Our small Tuesday afternoon department store audience rooted for my mother, wincing when one of the others stammered, cheering when my mother smilingly explained culinary terms, even though that meant she'd probably win less money.

"Okay, panelists," Bud Collyer interrupted, "it's time to vote. *Who*," he paused for emphasis, "do *YOU* think," pause, "is the *real*," pause, "*Elsie*," pause, his voice growing louder, "*MASTERTON?*" By now he was shouting. The camera panned back and forth showing my mother and the two fibbers' faces. "We'll be right back, after a word from our sponsors," and the picture on the screen shifted to a commercial for Geritol, boasting about how good it was "for iron-poor blood."

Even Daddy, I could see, was completely caught up, hardly looking away from the screen. Finally, after the commercial ended, the announcer's voice came booming from the television set, asking for each person's vote. Three of the four panelists voted for my mother. "And now," drum roll, "will the *real*," pause, "*Elsie*," pause, "*Masterton*," there was a long pause, "*please!*" pause, "*STAND UP!!!*"

My mother and the other two women shifted around in their chairs, one of the fakes almost standing up but ultimately sitting back down as my mother pushed back her chair, looked at the other two women, and came to a full standing position. Everyone was smiling. The studio audience clapped. And there, in the Economy Department Store, our gathered group applauded. Daddy blew his nose in pleasure, which meant, I knew, that he had been crying. I almost exploded with pride, and I didn't even care about her not fooling people.

Bud Collyer went over to my mother, led her to the panelists, who shook her hand, and then introduced the two imposters: a housewife and a secretary. Bud, my mother, the panelists, and the imposters all stood around as the theme music played. Finally Bud turned my mother toward the camera. "And Elsie," he invited, "I understand you have something you'd like to say."

"Yes, thank you, Bud, I'd like to say hello to my daughters Lucinda and Laurey, who are watching in Vermont, to my daughter Heather, backstage with me here, and to my darling John, as always."

"She said hello! She said hello! Did you hear that? She said hello to me!" I ran around, screaming with delight.

"What say we go to the A+W and have root beer floats," my father said, guiding us back to the car. He parked in the lot of Rutland's very first drive-in restaurant, ordered the drinks, and tipped the waitress as she hooked the little tray onto the Citroën's window. I was, I thought to myself as I sipped my root beer float, the very luckiest of all the lucky slobs.

Chapter Eleven

Salmon Pea-Wiggle

 Most of the time when my mother and father went on a publicity trip I stayed with Miss Moore. But sometimes, especially later on, my sisters and I stayed with the Dwyers. Lucinda started going there when she was a baby, and, as Heather and I came along, we sometimes all stayed there. As they wrote more books, my parents went on more publicity trips and, not wanting to wear any one family out, they arranged for lots of different places for us to stay.

Elizabeth Dwyer cooked simple foods for us, giving us a very different culinary education from the one our parents offered. And, when our parents came home, we'd gleefully report on what we ate.

"Elizabeth gave us potato chips!" we exclaimed, coming home after a week with the Dwyers. "And she has a red *plastic* bowl! Can we have potato chips? Can we have a red plastic bowl? Can we? Can we?

"She made Salmon Pea-Wiggle, too! She puts it on saltines! Will you make us Salmon Pea-Wiggle? It's got salmon and peas and saltines! I'm sure Elizabeth would give you the recipe!"

"Put that one into your book, Mommy!" we pleaded, "Everyone would *love* it!"

Shockingly, or, should I say, to her credit, she did put the recipe in, grudgingly including a mention of this favorite food of ours. She gave it one paragraph in the "Pretty Kettle of Fish" chapter of *The Blueberry Hill Kitchen Notebook*. Here's my mother's recipe for Salmon Pea-Wiggle, just as she wrote it:

"I really shouldn't tell you about SALMON PEA-WIGGLE, I hate it so. But my children come home from the neighbors demanding it and decrying my cooking repertoire for not including it. It's canned salmon, drained. It's canned peas, drained. They're added to cream of mushroom soup. They're heated. That's salmon pea-wiggle."

And there's really not much more to say about that one.

Chapter Twelve

Steamed Hot Dogs at the Churchills'

 My sisters and I never wanted to spend time with all these other families. I do not ever remember asking to go to Miss Moore's or to the Dwyers' or, well, to anyone's home.

Actually, once, when I was in college, I went back to Miss Moore's for a night. She cooked dinner for me and told me stories about when I was little. "You were so adorable," she said, "with your dark curls sticking out from your snowsuit. You looked like an angel."

"Did I like coming here?" I asked her, remembering how much I had stayed with her.

"Well, yes," she said, "When you were about three, though, I took you up to the Inn for your birthday. At one point you came over to me, climbed up on my lap, and asked when we could go home. Your mother was in the room with us and heard you. She stopped bringing you here so much after that. You still came, but she took you home more often," her voice drifted off.

But our parents were busy. They needed to go back to New York to spread the word about Blueberry Hill. First both parents, and then later just my mother needed to go to meet with her publishers or to publicity events and cooking demonstrations. Her cookbooks did very well, but it meant that she was gone a lot. Much more than I liked.

And there were not that many people willing to take three girls. Three girls take up a lot of space and it's a lot to ask of a family. The Dwyers moved to Proctor and so were too far away. Miss Moore only had room for me. So we started staying with the Churchills.

George and Elise had a dairy farm in Forest Dale. Five miles from Blueberry Hill, right on Route 73, and close to our school, it was convenient for our parents to drop us off on their way to New York or Boston or wherever they went. George and Elise had one son, Peter, a strange boy who did not really talk. He sat with his face just inches from the television screen and watched cartoons or Westerns or the afternoon jazz show with his mouth gaping open. He poured grape juice on Sugar Smacks for his morning meal. He'd push the cereal box to me at breakfast but I remember thinking that if I ate that, I might turn out to be like him. After we stayed with the Churchills, I stopped wanting to watch television. We still didn't have one at home, but after a lot of time with the Churchills, I stopped thinking that was such a bad thing.

(One year, maybe the year I went back to visit Miss Moore, I heard that Peter had driven his go-kart out into the middle of that busy road and gotten hit by a truck. I'm still not sure if it is true, but we could tell, when we saw him sitting that close to the television, or when we watched him eating that sweet breakfast, that something bad might happen to him. I remember feeling very sad, though, when I heard what had happened. Peter was not a bad boy, just odd.)

George milked his twenty-four cows twice a day. Morning milking was done before any of the rest of us woke up. George would put on his knee-high black rubber boots and go out to the barn. Elise did not help, but stayed in the house, making toast and coffee and eggs. When my sisters and I got up there was always a big can of warm milk on the front step of the house, warm and ready for our breakfast. Sometimes, when their neighbors, the Wings, were home in their big house next to the Churchills, George would carry a can up to leave on their porch. But they didn't come up from Washington very much. Mostly we got all the milk.

I did not like warm milk. At home we had cold milk. And our milk came in cute, clean, glass bottles. We'd stop at Jennings' Dairy on the way home to the Inn from school. My mother would park the car and we'd heave open the huge walk-in refrigerator door in the garage behind the Jennings' house and fill up a metal carrier with bottles of pasteurized milk. My sisters and I got to mark the calendar with little tics for each bottle we took, and then we'd all get back into the car and drive up the mountain to Goshen. We passed the Churchills' farm every day and I always liked it more when we drove right by and did not have to stop and spend a night or a week or two weeks with them.

George was nice enough, though. He let me come with him to do the afternoon milking.

"Come Boss" he'd yell to the fields, and the cows would lumber in, swollen and fat with milk. "Come Boss." His voice sang the two notes of this song, his mouth slurring the words together so it sounded like "C'm boss," and rang out like a foghorn. The cows knew which stall they lived in and almost always went to the right place. Sometimes George had to slap one on the hind end. "Come Boss, you know where to go." George called all the cows Boss.

While George worked the milking machines, I skipped up and down the center aisle, careful to dance around the cow's tails and hooves. "They'll kick," George had warned on my first visit. I danced around the milk cans, inhaling the smells of the hay, the grain, the warm cows. George, finishing up a cow, milking by hand for the last drops of milk, would squirt a steaming stream into a poised cat's mouth. "Want some?" he'd chuckle, glancing at me.

"*No!*" I'd yell. "Yuck!!"

On Sundays, the Churchills ate "dinner" right in the middle of the day. On Sundays no one ate breakfast, except for Peter, who slurped his usual bowl of Sugar Smacks and grape juice. No one at the Churchills' ate lunch on Sunday, either. And later there was no evening meal. George and Elise just ate this odd midday meal: Sunday dinner.

We did not eat Sunday dinner at Blueberry Hill. Our Sunday meals were pretty much like our other days' meals. We did not go to church, so there was nothing to go away and come home to, like some of my friend's families. And we did not have any grandparents, so we never went to their house to spend the day as a family, the way others of my friends did. In the winter time, we'd probably go skiing on a Sunday, but that did not involve any special meals. Sunday dinner was not part of my family's tradition. Later I would stay with people who cooked pot roast or roast beef or a whole baked chicken. And I learned how other families do their eating. But that was later. When I stayed with the Churchills, I did not know about Sunday dinner.

But Sunday dinner at the Churchills was no grand country feast. There was no pot roast. No roast beef. No chicken. Nope. Every single Sunday we ever stayed there, Elise served Steamed Hot Dogs. Steamed White Bread. Pickles. Baked Beans. Warm Milk. And that was it. Every Sunday. Okay, the pickles were good, but you can't make a whole meal out of pickles. At least I couldn't. I was always hungry on Sundays at the Churchills. Heather remembered the little metal holder that steamed the hot dogs on the inside and held the bread on the outside. Elise would bring this whole holder from the kitchen to the dining room table with her. It was interesting to look at—the first time—but it didn't make the food taste any better.

My sisters and I always wanted to go home sooner than we could. We did not want to be away as much as we were. I always missed home. I always missed my mother. I always missed our kitchen. I always missed my mother's food. Yes, in all ways I missed my home. No one I knew spent as much time with other families as we did. We put up with it, learning how to meld into these other places. During the week, when we stayed with other families, things were usually okay, since we continued to go to our schools like always. But the worst days, the worst days by far, were Sundays at the Churchills' when we had to eat Steamed Hot Dogs with White Bread and Pickles and Baked Beans from a can.

The Churchills don't live in that little white house on Route 73 anymore, I don't think, though I'm not really sure. Maybe they do. George's barn is falling in. The last time I went there I climbed around in the hay mow and blew huge clumps of dust off old carriages and farming machinery. The cows are long gone. The big house, the one next door to George and Elise's where the Wings used to come, is now a very fancy bed and breakfast. You can ski there from Blueberry Hill, if you want. "Inn-to-Inn Skiing." It's all very high end. Very spiff.

I wonder about George and Elise. Mostly I remember being so very relieved when we finally got to go home. It never came soon enough. And I never missed those hot dogs.

Chapter Thirteen

Mama's Sponge Cake with
Sour Cream Sauce and Hot Blueberries

 My favorite job at the Inn, when I was done shucking corn and peeling carrots, was being the dessert announcer. I was too small and too young to serve the guests, though that was not *my* decision. As far as I was concerned, I could operate the entire Inn, even if I was still just a kid. At the age of seven, I became the dessert announcer.

When dinner was done, the dinner plates cleared, and the guests' conversations had started up once again after the quiet concentration that comes with eating, my mother and I would roll the buffet table back into the dining room. She would have cleared off the Roast Beef and the Tomatoes Seven Seasonings and the Brussels Sprouts with Green Grapes and would have filled the table with desserts, made by her that very afternoon. We'd stand at the front of the room, right in front of the big stone fireplace, and, after waiting for the guests' attention, and invited by my mother, I would start to speak.

"For dessert this evening we have Fruit Compote in Wine, Apple Nut 'Thing,' Chocolate Pound Cake with Rum Whipped Cream," I'd announce, glancing back at the dessert table to remind myself, "and Mama's Sponge Cake with Sour Cream Sauce and Hot Blueberries."

My mother, out of the kitchen after a day of cooking, and clean in a fresh red-checked shirt, stood next to me and prompted if I lost my place or forgot one of the items. Her face, washed, always looked soft to me, but by dessert I could see she was tired after her long, hot day. Still, she watched, proud, as I went through the list each night.

"And Miracle Meringue Cake," she'd whisper.

"Oh, and Miracle Meringue Cake," I'd add.

This was a performance to me, a singular moment in a small spotlight. It was my job, exclusively. I was in training, I felt, practicing for the time when I would run Blueberry Hill. This, I knew, would surely happen one day.

And then, just as my father had done, my mother went around the dining room, asking one guest at a time for their dessert choice, carefully presenting it on a plate, and giving it to one of the college girls to serve. Another waitress served coffee. I retreated to the kitchen to see if there were any leftover Tomatoes Seven Seasonings to eat.

Mama's Sponge Cake with Sour Cream Sauce and Hot Blueberries was the favorite, the specialty of the house. Mama was my mother's mother and her sponge cake, made with orange juice, was a connection to my mother's past. How comforting it must have been for her to mix those ingredients every single afternoon, baking this reminder of her childhood. Mama made her sponge cake into jelly rolls, trifles, birthday cakes, and probably cupcakes, too. My mother just made this simple sponge cake. It was perfect just as it was and appeared on the dessert table every night.

When I started cooking for a living, and needed a special dessert one night, I remembered Mama's Sponge Cake with Sour Cream Sauce and Hot Blueberries. And, though it had been more than twenty years since we'd served the last dinner at the Inn, the recipe worked perfectly in my kitchen and the guests—my guests this time—ate with quiet pleasure.

I'm serving a dinner party in a week and have suggested Mama's Sponge Cake with Sour Cream Sauce and Hot Blueberries (have you noticed yet that I have to say the entire name of this cake, sauce and all?). I look forward to bringing this bit of my mother and her mother to these guests. And I love being me, now, age forty-nine, saying, "For dessert this evening we have Mama's Sponge Cake with Sour Cream Sauce and Hot Blueberries." Makes me smile.

Mama's Sponge Cake with
Sour Cream Sauce and Hot Blueberries
The Recipe

My grandmother made this cake for every possible cake occasion there was. Sometimes she'd make it in a jelly roll pan, fill it with whipped cream and fruit, and roll it up. And sometimes she'd tear leftover cake into chunks and make a trifle-like dessert with it. But at Blueberry Hill our guests never could get enough of it served with this simple sour cream sauce and hot blueberries. I've served it at many dinner parties. People still love it and are pleased with how light it is. You know, they get a sweet finish without all the hoopla that goes with many desserts these days.

I'm going to give you the recipe as my mother wrote it. No changes are needed. Here you go.

Serves 12 easily

The ingredients:

4 large eggs
1 cup sugar
½ cup orange juice

1 cup all purpose flour
1 teaspoon baking powder

Here's what you do: Separate the eggs and set aside the whites. Beat the egg yolks until light and lemon-colored. Add sugar and beat until granular consistency disappears (about 3 minutes at medium speed in the electric mixer.) Add orange juice, beating until well mixed, then continue for 2 minutes more. Sift together the flour and baking powder. Add to egg mixture and beat until thoroughly assimilated, then another 2 minutes.

Beat the egg whites until stiff, but not dry. Fold whites into rest of batter, carefully, until no specks of white are seen. Turn batter into an angel food pan. Bake in a moderate (325°F) oven for 30 to 40 minutes, or until the cake pops back into shape when you touch it firmly with your finger.

(This cake will not rise to the top of a regular angel food pan. If you want it that large, use 6 eggs and multiply everything else by 1 ½).

For the Sour Cream Sauce, mix 1 pint of sour cream with 1 tablespoon of sugar and 1 teaspoon of pure vanilla. A fork is fine here. Just stir until blended.

And, for the Hot Blueberry Sauce, put 2 cups of fresh berries in a small saucepan with 1 tablespoon of lemon juice, ½ cup of sugar and ½ cup water. Bring to a boil and let boil for 2 minutes. If it is too watery, let it cook for 4 or 5 more minutes to thicken it up just a bit. Taste for sugar and lemon. Tart berries will need more. Adjust to suit your taste.

To make a thicker sauce, dissolve 1 teaspoon of cornstarch in ½ cup cold water. Stir it around with a fork until it is very smooth and then add it to the cooked berry mixture, letting it boil for another minute.

To serve: Slice the cake with a serrated knife. Place a slice on a dessert plate. Give a good dollop (a fat tablespoon or so) of Sour Cream Sauce, to each serving of cake. And then, right before serving, ladle a hearty spoonful of the hot blueberries over the sour cream, letting some drip onto the cake.

Chapter Fourteen

Trout Fishing

 It is spring here in the mountains and I can't stop thinking about trout. Trout fishing. Trout cooking. Trout eating. Yes, here in North Carolina it is now fully spring. Daffodils dance on top of their green stalks. Crocus peaked over a month ago. Tulips will pop open any day now, and the peas, planted here on St. Patrick's Day, are pushing up through the dark soil, still green and small but promising meals and sweetly crunchy bites in just a few weeks.

In Vermont right now, I suspect things are different. They must be stuck in the middle of "mud season" by now, one of two additional seasons they get to endure: mud season and black fly season. Ugh. I don't miss *that*! In early spring, our Vermont dirt roads froze at night and then thawed with the sun. Up in Goshen, the roads rutted in huge, deep crater-like pits which were made worse by the logging trucks. The forests around Blueberry Hill were logged and serviced by huge hulks of trucks that carried off the fat tree trunks. Mountainside-cut trees were too difficult to reach with trucks in those gentler days, before clear-cutting, so each morning the loggers harnessed Roxy, a gigantic Belgian workhorse, and led her up Hogback Mountain, right behind Blueberry Hill, to drag their felled logs down to the flatbeds waiting to drive down The Big Hill to the lumber mills in town.

For me, the first day of spring was always the day when the birds returned. Big, fat blue jays called out for the first time on that day each year. If they sang before then, I never heard them. To me, that first day of spring was also the first day of fishing. From an official point of view, the opening of Trout Season was probably on some other day but I was eight and our brook was tucked up behind the Inn far from any game warden, so I didn't care much about licenses and Official Trout Seasons and such.

My fishing expeditions started at the manure pile next to the barn. Five minutes with a pitchfork and a can set me up nicely for a day at the brook, yielding enough fat worms to last a whole day. Some grown ups suggested I sneak up on the fish, hiding from them, getting close, but not so close as to reveal my position. I preferred the more rambunctious approach, hooking a fish from the bridge twenty feet above the brook, and trying to reel it up, watching as it wriggled out of the water, careened through air, and then inevitably fell off just inches short of my reach.

"Why don't you fish down beside the brook?" an adult might suggest. "You'd probably get to keep a fish or two if you got closer to the water."

But that was not a much of a challenge for me. I sat, perched and impatient but very happy from my lookout up on top of the culvert. I did not bring many fish home. And that didn't matter.

One day, my half sister's husband Rod came to take me fishing. We didn't see my father's other two daughters that much, but when they did come, I looked forward to fishing with my half brother-in-law. Rod took me down the brook as far as the old beaver dam where the water, which was gurgling and active near the Inn, spread out and grew still. Rod stood on one side of the brook, I took up a spot on the other. I had put a couple of extra worms in my pocket and, once settled in my spot, put one on my hook and tossed the line into the water. Rod coached me to stand back from the bank, "so they won't see you," but I liked to watch for fish so I stayed close to the edge.

"Say, Squirt," he spoke after ten minutes of quiet fishing, "Toss me another worm. I'm out." (By the way, fly-fishing in that brook was out of the question. The maples and birches hovered over the water and made casting impossible. People from out of state did fly-fishing. We, wanting fish, used worms.)

Instead of tossing Rod one or two worms, I waded across the brook, getting completely wet all the way up to my chest. Rod shook his head, watching my enthusiastic grin. "Squirt," he said, "you are something else."

Rod cast his line into the dark corners of every fishing hole. I was much clumsier, heaving a lead-weighted, worm-wrapped hook as close to the fish as I could manage. Rod caught a lot of fish. Most times I did not.

On that day I filled my pockets with fish, stuffing them in, and then, when there were too many because Rod gave me all of his, stringing them on a fresh-cut stick which I carried all the way home. I felt like I was in an adventure story and we had just collected our night's dinner. We were victorious!

Back at the Inn, my mother cleaned our fish, first snipping the fins and gills with her red-handled scissors and then quickly cleaning out the insides. Fish that fresh glisten and smell like new grass. She heated butter in a cast-iron frying pan, rolled my fish ("These're *just* barely legal," Rod had said) in a little bit of corn meal and flour and sprinkled them with a shake of salt and pepper.

"You two sit," she instructed, "These'll be done in a minute."

When Uncle Rob, my mother's favorite neighbor, was alive, way before I was born, my mother cooked his trout for him this way, adding steamed, just-cut fiddlehead fern tops or pencil-thin asparagus. For Rod and me, my mother just made trout, drizzling them with a squeeze of lemon and a shred of fresh dill before plunking them on a plate. Rod winked at me as we shared our catch with my mother, "Pretty good, for a squirt."

Laurey's "Cold Mountain" Smoked Trout Mousse
The Recipe

Here in the mountains of North Carolina we live almost within shouting distance of Cold Mountain. Clear water, clean air, all of this helps produce the trout we use at Laurey's Catering. Sometimes we smoke our own, but Dick Jennings, over at Sunburst Trout Company (which also produces the best domestic caviar in the United States, as judged by the folks at *Gourmet* magazine) has just come up with a delicious, consistent, cold-smoked fillet, which we have been turning into Smoked Trout Mousse. It is one of our new favorite things to bring to parties. If you're not lucky enough to come here and taste ours, feel free to adapt this recipe with local smoked fish from your area. Here's our recipe, developed by Deb here in our kitchens. The folks at Sunburst Trout Farms liked it so much they asked for the recipe. We thought that pretty flattering. Wouldn't you?

Makes about 8 cups

The ingredients:

2 pounds cream cheese
  (four 8-ounce packages)
4 cups ricotta cheese
2 tablespoons fresh lemon juice
1/4 cup grated horseradish
  (more or less to taste)

1 teaspoon onion powder
4 shots Tabasco sauce
1/4 cup chopped fresh dill
8 ounces Sunburst Trout Cold Smoked
  Trout fillets, skinned and cut into
  1/2-inch strips

Here's what you do: Combine all the ingredients except for the trout in the bowl of a food processor. Process with the steel blade until smooth. Add the trout pieces and pulse just until the trout is in a rough puree. In the final mix, some texture is good, so don't get carried away, all right?

Chill and serve with fresh vegetables, crackers, or sliced toasted sourdough baguette rounds.

By the way, I'm sure I know what you'll say, but let me know what you think, okay?

Chapter Fifteen

Steak for Breakfast

 We did not serve steak at Blueberry Hill.

Just the other day, I was telling stories to Mark, the baker at work. We had had a particularly pesky party the night before, with irritating clients who ordered us around like we were servants from another era. They reminded me of one guest from the Inn.

"This woman brought enough steaks so her *dog* could eat one every single night of her two-week stay," I recounted. "And she made my mother pan-fry them with just the right amount of seasoning. She'd stand right next to the stove, vigilant, watching over my mother's shoulder. Too much salt or too little pepper and the dog wouldn't eat."

My mother, I remember, did what the guest wanted, but she was not amused. A whole steak for a dog? And each night for two whole weeks?

My mother preferred making things that took some artistry. Lamb, roasted with coffee and mustard and brown sugar. Thick fillets of cod, smothered in sour cream and sweet onions, oregano, and a splash of white wine. We had a couple of Caribbean grills called "hot pots" that stayed in the living room fireplace all winter, waiting for the occasional midwinter grill. We grilled Shish Kebobs on them, long-marinated in lemon and fresh herbs. We never grilled, or served, plain steak.

But one time my mother and both sisters were away on a trip in New York.

"Let's have steak for dinner," my father suggested, his eyes twinkling. "Just steak. Just you and me."

We drove to Brandon, me in the passenger seat, paying close attention to my father's driving, making sure to shift my grape soda bottle "gearshift" whenever he did, and steering with an imaginary steering wheel. In nine years I would get my driver's license. It was important to be ready.

At the Grand Union, my father bought us a big steak. On the way home, we stopped at Brown's Pharmacy, where he got us each an ice cream cone: vanilla for me, pistachio for him. Dessert first, then dinner, why not? He winked at me, sharing the pleasure. When ice cream dripped down my arm he took my cone, licked it to catch the drips, and handed it back.

At home he broiled our steak, put it on a plate, set it on the table and, right off the plate, we ate. Well, we ate part of it. It was big enough for two more of us, I'd say, so when we were full, he wrapped up the leftovers, put the package in the refrigerator and read to me from my favorite book, *The Night Mother Was Away*.

In the book, a little girl and her father spend the night at home without the mother, who has gone on a trip. It does not say where the mother is. The little girl can't sleep, so the father takes her for a walk in the moonlight. I thought of that story as I lay in bed. I missed my mother and my sisters, but, full of steak and happy to be home with just my father that night, I drifted to sleep.

In the morning we ate our leftover steak. I made us some fried eggs, which, even at eight, I could do pretty well. He made Sanka for himself and poured me some juice. He read the paper. I looked around the kitchen, musing on cooking and steak and my father.

I am the youngest of my father's five daughters, the last child who did not get to be named John Ferguson Masterton II. Patsy and Diane are his daughters from his first marriage. And in my family there are Lucinda, Heather, and me. Deciding, as he did with Diane, that it didn't really matter if he had another girl instead of his hoped-for boy, my father took me under his wing and included me in traditional father-and-son activities. He took me to the stock car races, taught me to play pool, gave me my first taste of beer at the ripe old age of eight, and built model cars, planes, and trains with me. But "don't you ever let me catch you smoking," he warned, "or I'll break you arm." (Not really, I knew, but I got the message.) He smoked. But we were not to. He made it very clear.

He was the strict disciplinarian. "Don't talk with your mouth full," he'd bark, and "Don't derrick your food," he'd scold, if we reached too far for second helpings from a far away platter. But he was also the one to let us in on tastes of a world that we might otherwise have missed. I don't think that they planned it this way, but, in contrast to my mother's elegant cooking, my father was the one who introduced me and my sisters to a much more casual cuisine.

"Don't tell Mommy," he'd say as he bought us cotton candy, hot dogs—fair food from tattooed vendors. "This will just be *our* little secret." We'd giggle, taste, laugh with him. "One

Manhattan," he'd order from the waitress when we were out to dinner, "and please give us three cherries."

He gave me golf lessons one year, hoping I'd grow into a golf mate. My ten-year-old body hated the agonizingly slow walking from hole to hole. My dark hair, accustomed to the shade of a treehouse or the cool dark of a secret hideout in a cave by the brook, burned in the sun. I put up with these golf outings because he invited me, of course, but more important, because the end of the game meant the glorious reward of an ice-cold grape soda and a package of cheese-peanut butter crackers. Nothing like 'em!

So yes, steak for breakfast. Simple food. Simple memories. It takes plain and fancy to make an interesting life. I'm glad I had both.

Chapter Sixteen

TV Dinners . . . Shhh!

Even a gourmet cook gets tired of fancy food. My mother was no exception. And while she traveled to New York a few times a year and made a point to have lovely meals in fine restaurants, she also had her own comfort foods which she ate when she was tired: Cream of Wheat cereal, Maple Walnut Ice Cream with Maple Syrup, leftovers of many kinds. But, like any cook at one time or other, she was curious about the pre-made, packaged dinners that were becoming popular then, right along with the popularity of television.

We did not have TV, however, so a "TV dinner" was completely out of the question. That is, the idea of heating up a frozen dinner and sitting in front of a television with a little aluminum tray on an individual table was *not* something my mother would have put up with even if we *did* have a TV. Yes, as I said, she did rent one for us for special television occasions, but just because we didn't have a TV didn't mean she wasn't curious about TV dinners.

I, on the other hand, thought they were a great idea, and I mentioned them at any chance I could find, suggesting we "just try" them. The pictures looked so good on those cute little boxes with their little divided trays, little wisps of steam rising from the perfect little neat compartments of meats and potatoes. As my mother discussed orders of Roast Beef with the butcher at the grocery store, Heather and I pored over the descriptions in the freezer section.

"Mmm! Apple Brown Betty, *that* looks good!"

"This one has chocolate pudding!"

"Look! Mashed potatoes and gravy and three pieces of deep-fried chicken!"

"Can we, Mommy? Can we?"

My mother herded us into the car, sputtering about how she *knew* she should not have brought us into the A&P. But we had seen her eyeing the boxes too. It was hard not to wonder about how "delicious and convenient" they would be.

"Okay," she said one day when we were in Middlebury for violin lessons, "we'll try them this once. And," I heard her mutter under her breath, "I hope no one sees us!" It would not be right, she told us, for Elsie Masterton of Blueberry Hill to be buying frozen TV dinners. We had to be quick and if we saw anyone we knew, well, we just hoped that didn't happen.

We scampered into the Grand Union, skipped over to the frozen food case, and picked out five boxes, one for each of us and one for our father. We discussed and pondered our choices, methodically selecting the right mix so we could try the greatest variety of meals.

"Do you think Daddy would like Roast Beef or Meatloaf better?" we wondered.

"I'm going to get Beef Pot Pie!"

"Look, Turkey with stuffing *and* cranberry sauce *and* mashed potatoes *and* green beans *and* pumpkin pie! Let's get him that one!"

We shopped a bit more, my mother hastily stacking other acceptable groceries on top of the telltale narrow green boxed dinners: First Prize sausage, Chock Full O' Nuts coffee, Domino brown sugar, whole cranberries, eggs—all "raw" ingredients, nothing "prepared" about them.

We couldn't wait to get home, urging my mother to drive faster than usual through the ribbons of turns alongside the river on the Ripton Road. The leaves, slick from a fall rain, glistened, covered the river, foretold winter. And we were having TV dinners! I was very excited.

At home my sisters and I helped unload the car, put away the groceries, even volunteered to practice for our violin lessons without extra coaxing. TV dinners!

My mother opened all the boxes, turned on the oven, peeled back the little foil covers for the things that needed to have their little foil covers peeled back, left the little aluminum covers on the things that needed to stay covered, and put our dinners on the racks in the oven.

I sat and watched through the oven door, not that there was much to see—little aluminum trays with bland looking lumps in little sections of foil. Heather set the table, and Lucinda, a bit too sophisticated to get excited about TV dinners, went to her room to draw a picture of a horse's anatomy for her entry in the ninth grade science fair.

It did seem odd that the kitchen counters were so clean, except for the pile of boxes. The room did not really fill up with the aroma of onions and garlic, wine and spice, which made it seem lonely in an odd way. And it was strange to have nothing, really, to do, while we waited. My mother just looked at the oven. At a certain point a timer rang. The directions on the box said to peel back the little covered dessert areas, which we did. And then, a few minutes later, dinner was ready. Heather and I carried the little trays to the table, me still jumping around, happily chirping, "TV dinners! TV dinners! TV dinners!" Heather, a bit more reserved, acted as if she didn't really care that much, but I could tell she did. Lucinda, engrossed in her drawing, came down to the dining room, distracted and mostly interested, I could see, in getting back to her project. Still, when we could, we ate dinner together in my family, so she joined the rest of us.

My father, called from the living room, came in, sat down, looked over the top of his glasses, stopped, lifted his glasses up over his nose, looked up at my mother, put his glasses back down onto his nose, picked up his fork and pushed the little mound of turkey to one side of the little triangular partition in his tray. He looked back up at my mother, noticing the little trays at all our places. His eyebrows lifted as if to say, "What is *this*?"

My mother shrugged, "We thought we should try them, darling," and she too picked up her fork.

To no one's surprise but mine, the dinners were all awful. The chicken was either hard or mushy. The green beans tasted like dishwater. The turkey slices were like little slabs of cardboard. And I burned my tongue on the Apple Brown Betty. As it turned out, none of us, after the first taste, wanted any more.

"These are terrible!"

"Mine tastes awful!"

"This chicken is like rubber!"

"Yuck!"

Maybe they would have tasted better if we had had the distraction of TV. But, since we didn't, there was no hiding the truth that this was just plain bad food. We all, one at a time, put our forks down.

"Let's make pancakes, darling," my father suggested. "Let's just put this stuff out for the raccoons and make pancakes."

And so we did.

Chapter Seventeen

Fourth of July

I skipped the fireworks this year. I have a new puppy who, I felt, would not appreciate the booming and popping and jarring noise of it all. And, since I needed to get up early the next day for work, I took my pup home, where we sat on the porch and watched fireflies in the dusk. When night came, we heard explosions way over the hills and saw the sky light up. My neighbors set off little crackly things and lit some small fireworks too, so we had our own private show.

At Blueberry Hill, on the Fourth of July, my focus was always to wish everyone would get through dinner as fast as possible so we could pile into the car and drive to town, eight miles away, for the fireworks show. The Brandon Training School had big fields and everyone drove in, parked where the flashlight-toting men directed and, headlights off, waited.

In order for me to get to stay up late on the Fourth of July, I would have to take a nap earlier in the afternoon, which was nearly impossible, since I had such enormous excitement about the evening. Heather and Lucinda, eight and ten, were old enough to stay up, but I still needed quiet time, even though I fought hard against this rule. I lay in bed counting to myself. "One, two, three . . . is it time yet? Four, five, six . . . is it time yet?"

"Don't forget about the finale!" Heather had danced around, reminding me. It sounded like she was saying "fin-AL-ly" and I quivered with excitement. "You remember the finale!" she whispered. "All those colors! It's almost time!"

As the afternoon crawled on, everyone pitched in to get everything ready for the night's dinner. Amazingly, my mother cooked and baked everything alone every single night. Now, as I do the work I do, I think about her making every single part of every night's dinner. She did have help in the summer, but on most days it was she who drove to Brandon, shopped for fresh produce and cut-to-order meats, and then came back and spent the afternoon cooking and baking for the guests. On the Fourth of July, it all felt excruciatingly slow to me. And though I loved helping, on that day I was a fidgety ball of energy and, as far as I was concerned, the clock had stopped.

Finally, as the sun started to set, guests began to arrive. As if in slow motion they parked, strolled around the lawn admiring the phlox and the snapdragons and the blueberries, and wandered into the Inn. At a snail's pace, my mother cooked Shrimp Tempura and then, at a crawl it seemed, the guests got up, moved into the dining room, and, one guest at a time, helped themselves to my sister's offerings of my mother's salad and her tiny Sour Cream Biscuits served with her Blueberry Jam.

Would this dinner ever get finished? I squirmed.

Right on grown-up schedule, my mother arranged Chicken Baked in Wine, Noodles with Sherry, Tomatoes Seven Seasonings, and Broccoli Drizzled with Browned Butter on my father's serving cart and, ever so slowly (argh!!!) he rolled it into the dining room. Serving one guest at a time ("What's the rush?" his motions seemed to say) he made his way around the dining room. The twenty-five guests were there for dinner and no one but me was thinking of fireworks.

As the sky darkened at the end of this endless summer day, and after the guests had sampled my mother's dessert table of Mama's Sponge Cake with Sour Cream Sauce and Hot Blueberries, Apple Nut "Thing," Fruit Compote in Wine, or Blueberry Apple Crisp, the adults finally acknowledged it was time to leave to go to watch the fireworks. Guests, and some of the summer help, piled into the cars with us and we raced down the dirt roads to Brandon just as the final bit of light faded out of the summer sky.

As soon as we parked, the show started. Brandon only had a few thousand residents but the small show was perfect for us. A string of Roman candles led off. A few red oval rings of stars flashed, some screaming orange things whirled around us, dropping tiny cinders onto our heads. I burrowed into my mother's lap, waiting for those painful white ka-BLAM things that usually made me cry. As the show continued, I grew sleepy. And then, barely awake, the firemen lit the fuses for the finale ("the fin-AL-ly, the fin-AL-ly!" Heather yelped) which, in Brandon, was a minute-long rush of noise and color and one flash on top of another. I never remembered my father driving us home or getting out of my clothes and into my pajamas, but somehow the next morning, that's where I'd be.

Things then were perfect.

I've been gone from Vermont for a long time now and I've seen a number of spectacular fireworks displays. I lived in New York City the year the Brooklyn Bridge had a birthday party and *that* was a show! I stood on the shore of the East River, right next to the bridge, and screamed with the throngs as explosion after explosion erupted over our heads. The famous Grucci family put on that show and it was utterly magnificent. But the small-time shows from Brandon remain sweet in my dreams.

The other night, the night after the Fourth that my puppy and I missed, I drove with her to visit a couple of friends for dinner up north of here. On the way home, just at the time when all the afternoon light had faded into the night, and just as I arrived at a small town near my friends' home, the sky lit up! Fireworks! But wait, this was July 5th!! And no, this was no chance neighbor blowing up a leftover firework—this was the real thing, the town's festivities postponed from Friday the 4th until the more convenient Saturday this year. What fun! Fireworks. I couldn't resist.

I pulled over to the side of the road, watching my puppy to be sure she was not going to be terrorized by the noise, and, when it was clear that she was intrigued but not scared, I turned off the engine and we sat back and had a world class view of this small town's show. They started with a few warm-up Roman candles and gradually added in some red oval rings of stars. They had a few of those funny screaming orange things and they had the requisite booming white explosions too. My puppy fell asleep (so much for worrying!) and I had the all the time I wanted to remember.

I had a half-hour drive ahead of me, though, so as soon as the finale was over ("fin-AL-ly, fin-AL-ly, fin-AL-ly!" I could hear Heather saying) I started the engine, drove home, put on my pajamas, and fell asleep dreaming of Chicken Baked in Wine and being in a hurry to get to Brandon.

Chapter Eighteen

Little Packets of Jelly

 Funny. You'd think I'd have clearer memories of those next months. You'd guess that my mind would be full of pictures and smells and tastes and thoughts and conversations. But it isn't. I mostly just remember the little packets of jelly. And I remember that we didn't have any warning.

My parents had been in the hospital since September. Just before they left Vermont, my mother had arranged for a friend, a regular Inn guest, to come stay with me and Heather at the Brandon Inn, just for a week or so. My mother and father were off to see the doctor in Boston, they had told us. He, a smoker, needed treatment for pneumonia, which he got every year the same way most people get colds. She had had cancer some years before and was, she said, going along to get a checkup. Now I realize that was probably not the truth, but what do you say to children?

Lucinda was in boarding school in Massachusetts. Heather, in eighth grade and I, in sixth, moved from Blueberry Hill to the Brandon Inn for two weeks. By then the Dwyers had moved away, Miss Moore was not well, and the Churchills were not able to take us in.

"Just two weeks, Sweetie Pie," our mother had said. Heather and I had read *Eloise* and we had stayed at fancy hotels with our mother when we'd gone with her on publicity trips, so we knew how to sit, order from a menu, be polite. And the guest from the Inn was with us, joining us at the dinner table, making sure we got up in time to go to school, checking to see if we needed help with our homework. But after a short time, after the two weeks were over, someone decided that it was too expensive for us to stay in hotel rooms, ordering breakfast and dinner from the menu. It was clear that our parents were not coming home any time soon and that we would have to live somewhere different.

Someone, whoever it was that was helping my mother and father make the decisions, called and arranged for us to stay at the home of the people who answered Blueberry Hill's telephones when we were away at various times of the year. Joan and Bob Thomas had two young children and a small house, but they managed to find room for me and Heather. Linda, the daughter, moved her Barbie Doll Dream House and Bob put two cots in the corner of

Linda's room for us. Joan hung a curtain in front of the tiny upstairs bathroom and Robbie, the son, cleaned up his toys. Heather and I moved in.

October passed. Heather rode the bus to the Otter Valley Regional High School with her friend Nell. I walked down the hill with the kids in the neighborhood to the Brandon Grade School. On the weekends, Heather stayed with Nell and I played with the neighborhood kids. That fall we built an elaborate land with castles and rules and hidden places. We sculpted jumps, preparing for the winter and skiing. We constructed forts, calling our creation "The Green Hills Far Away." Lee, the neighbor's oldest son, and I read a lot of German prison camp books that fall and everyone in the neighborhood joined in and built lookout towers in the pine trees near the power station up at the base of Mount Pleasant. We hiked up to the Tea House at the top of the hill. Sometimes we snuck into the Kittel boys' treehouse, feeling invincible as we surveyed our territory. Our cheeks were perpetually pink. We glowed, radiant and healthy from our constant motion. In school, Mr. Johnson taught us science and math and history. We got a new student in my class who was cuter and smarter and presented a new threat to me. I was now one of the top three instead of one of the top two students. I wrote all of this in letters to my mother, far away in the hospital in Boston, trying to tell her what I was doing. We called on Sunday mornings.

"Hi, Pumpkin," she'd say faintly "how are you?"

And I'd tell her about the forts and the jumps and Mr. Johnson and Sally, the cute, smart new girl in my class.

In November in Vermont things change. Leaves, dazzling for a week at the end of September and the beginning of October, fall off the trees and the landscape becomes grey and bare. Someone, whoever was making the decisions, decided that Heather and I would go to Boston for a weekend to visit. It was almost Thanksgiving, but no one felt that it was time for us all to go home. Not yet.

Lucinda took a bus to Boston from her school. Heather and I were driven down. I think there was a snowstorm. Roz and Brayton Lincoln, frequent guests at the Inn, had arranged for us to all go to the Ice Capades. But that was going to happen on Saturday. It was just Friday.

Someone, whoever was in charge, led us into the hospital room. My mother sat up in bed. She looked so tired. The walls of the room were pale yellow. Who decides to paint the walls of the hospital room yellow? I'd heard the word "jaundice," and knew that it meant a person who was so sick she was yellow. Was it jaundice I was seeing or paint? The walls of my mother's room were filled with our pictures and cards and letters. Her windowsill was covered with vases of flowers and plants. Cards stuck out of the pots with soft words of hope. As we walked in, my mother stopped sorting through shoe boxes filled with greeting cards. Hundreds and hundreds of listeners from her *Farm Paper of the Air* radio program had flooded her room with notes of sympathy when the radio station had announced she was ill. She looked up at us, her hands still in the box of cards. We shook off the hands of the adult who'd led us in, and ran, falling on her bed, on top of her, hugging and hugging and squealing, holding on as if we would never ever let go.

My father came up from his room on the floor below hers, dressed in a bathrobe and slippers, helped by another friend, another guest from the Inn. He looked so thin, tired, pale. But he smiled, relaxed, pleased that we were all together again. We all sat on our mother's bed, telling stories and being a family in the odd yellow room with all the cards and flowers.

And then someone, whoever it was who was saying these things, said, "Okay, girls, your mother looks tired, so let's give her time for a nap and we'll go to the cafeteria and get a snack, shall we?"

The linoleum floor of the hospital had colors imbedded in the tiles. "Follow the Red Line to the South Annex," a sign said. "Follow blue to the solarium. Green to the cafeteria." I wondered where the orange, the purple, the black led. We followed the green lines into the elevator, and, once in the basement, under the streets of Boston, through low corridors with hissing pipes and strange beeping bells. Faint voices paged doctors. We hurried along. The orange line split off. So did the purple. The black. Finally we were just following the green.

The cafeteria was small. Clearly people did not spend long periods of time in this place. There was one room that held just four square, brown tables. A salt and pepper shaker and a red plastic bottle of ketchup sat on each table. A trash can stood next to the door which opened into the room with the food. A small black sign with those little white removable letters listed the menu:

> Eggs: hard-boiled or scrambled. White Toast with Butter and Jelly. Bacon. Orange Juice. Grapefruit Juice. Coffee. Tea. Cereal. Breakfast served all day. Lunch served from 12:00–2:00. Dinner served from 5–7. Please place order at the counter. Have a nice day.

We looked at the sign. We were not hungry, but we had to stay there in the small cafeteria, at least for a while, so we figured we might as well order something. I looked up at the man behind the glass partition. On the top of the partition was a shelf, and on it was a basket filled with cute, bright little packets of jelly. I had never seen anything like them. Little individual servings of jelly in cute little rectangular packages. I looked at the basket.

The man winked at me, "Go ahead! Take a look! You can have any one you choose. Take your pick! And how 'bout some toast and scrambled eggs, young lady?"

I blinked, breathed. "Yes, please" I said, staring at the basket of little packets of jelly, forgetting that I hated scrambled eggs.

Whoever was paying took care of the bill and my sisters and I went to the other room, carrying our food on brown plastic trays, and sat down. I looked at my tray, ignoring the toast, but fascinated by the little packets of jelly. I had taken two, hoping that I would not get in trouble. Grape. And mixed fruit. I had not chosen the orange marmalade or the boysenberry or the apple or the strawberry, though it was hard to decide. I liked grape soda, so maybe, I hoped, this would be like that. And the picture on the outside of the mixed fruit jelly was inviting: blackberries and raspberries and strawberries. Ignoring my eggs, I peeled back the covers on the two little packets of jelly. I took my knife and spread some on the toast, a little bit of each on opposite corners of the browned white bread. The only jam I'd ever eaten before that was my mother's Blueberry Jam, which she and my father made every summer from berries we picked in the blueberry patch at the side of the Inn. They made Cranberry Relish too. And Cucumber Marmalade. Big vats of each—steaming jars and lots of bustle and speed to get the jams canned and labeled and sold and shipped. We sent the jam all over the United States. Fancy stores sold it. At one point it was featured in the windows of Rockefeller Center. And, for a time, my parents' jams had been sold in Altman's, which for two people in a small place in Vermont, was a very big deal.

The jellies in the little packets on my tray were very sweet. I closed my eyes and tasted. Which was the grape? I tested myself. Which was the mixed fruit? And why, I wondered, could I not tell the difference.

"Okay, Laurey, let's go." My experimenting was interrupted and whoever it was that was in charge showed us how to clear our trays and helped us follow the colors in the floor back to our mother's room. My father had gone back to his room and my mother was sleeping. I had wanted to tell her about the little packets of jelly, but went along with the adult who told us we had to leave.

We stayed in Boston for a whole weekend. We did go to the Ice Capades with the Lincolns. I don't remember a bit of it. We did have some sort of a Thanksgiving dinner, on Sunday, I think. We must have. It was Thanksgiving time, even though we were not in Vermont and my mother had not cooked and it was not even Thursday. I don't remember very much else.

But I do remember running through those steamy corridors, following the lines in the floor, going back again and again to the cafeteria. After that first trip, the people who were making decisions let us go alone and every time we had to leave to let our mother take a nap, we'd follow the colors in the floor down to the cafeteria. I ordered toast every time, trying all the jellies, one flavor at a time. The man behind the counter finally told me I could take some with me if I wanted to, so I gathered up one of each flavor and took my collection back to Vermont where, at the Thomas' house, I put my little packets of jelly in a box which hid I under my cot in the corner of Linda's room. And I looked at them every day until my parents finally came home, right before Christmas.

Chapter Nineteen

Hay Hole Stew

 The day my father died was the day I learned how to make Hay Hole Stew. That third week of that July, the one of my twelfth year, was the week I learned how to cook outdoors. One hot day in late June, a woman who introduced herself as the director of a new Girl Scout day camp had knocked on our front door, asking my mother if she would agree to let them use our phone as an emergency calling site for a day camp they were going to hold starting the next week. By the end of the conversation with my mother, the director had noticed me peeking around the doorway and, before I knew it, they had enrolled me as a camper. I could hear whispered words about my father but they made sure to keep that part of the conversation from me.

Camp, the director said, would meet in the fields near the old gravel pit. We'd hike, swim, camp, and learn outdoor skills. We'd come home every night, so I would not get homesick like I had when I'd gone to sleep-away camp a couple of years before. This day camp arrangement sounded like fun to me.

My father was not doing well. He'd been sick with continual lung problems since November and, though finally well enough to be out of the hospital, he'd begun to slide away from us in late spring. By June, he was keeping all of us awake with nighttime speeches from his bed, loud conversations with people only he could see. Some nights we could hear him presenting arguments with an imagined judge from long-past lawsuits tried in his early days of working as a district attorney in Patterson, New Jersey. And during the afternoons we could see him sitting in one of the white Adirondack chairs out on the lawn, gesturing passionately at people—only there was never anyone standing where he was gesturing. Once a great driver, holder of a world record for outboard motor boat racing for five years, my mother had taken away his keys to the car after he'd turned up miles away from home one afternoon, having been gone for hours longer than he'd said he would. My father, by that July, had started to slip.

Camp would be a good way to get a twelve-year-old out of the house.

Much to my initial disappointment, a lot of Girl Scouts involved cooking. I guess they figured we girls would need to know how to cook if we were to make it on our own in the big world, not that that made much sense to me. I wanted to learn knife handling and gun cleaning, tourniquet making and treehouse construction or, frankly, anything practical. I had already learned a lot of those things on my own, poring through *Boy's Life* magazines in the Brandon library. I memorized first aid tips, preparing for the day when I would save someone's life and get memorialized in "A True Story of Scouts in Action," the feature I always studied first on my library trips. But those things, according to the Girls Scouts then, were for boys. We, at our Girl Scout day camp that summer, learned a whole lot about cooking.

On the first day of camp, we started by preparing the day's food. "Trail Mix" was a wonderful new food item for me: nuts, dried fruits, and M&M's, all swirled in a bag. What fun! Very easy, of course, but it was, after all, our first day. We hiked, ate, learned about knots, waded in the brook, played, hiked some more. Though not very thrilling, camp, I thought, might turn out to be fun.

Each night we all returned to our homes. Since he'd gotten really sick, I had learned to fix milk shakes for my father, but he was getting to the point where he was not interested in eating. I tried my best sitting on his bed with him, telling him stories of my day.

"We made Trail Mix today," I told him. "You put M&Ms and nuts and raisins in a bag and shake them up. That's it! Trail Mix!"

"Mmm hmm . . ." he murmured, his eyes remaining closed.

I hopped off to bed, tired from my day and eager to see what we would do at camp tomorrow.

The next day at camp, we went for a hike to the top of the gravel pit, picking pails full of blueberries. And that afternoon we learned how to make Pioneer Drumsticks: seasoned hamburger which we wadded onto the end of a stick, covered with sticky Bisquick mix, and cooked over a campfire. Though we dropped more meat than stuck onto our sticks, we congratulated ourselves at learning a more challenging recipe.

That afternoon I went back to the Inn, and back to my father.

"We learned Pioneer Drumsticks today, Daddy," I related. He barely nodded.

And then I returned to the kitchen to help as much as I could, scooping melon, helping toss the salad, arranging the biscuits. Upstairs my father drifted in and out of himself. And though I didn't really realize it then, we were losing him.

By midweek, we were getting more skilled at camp. We had a daytime cookout, finishing the meal with Banana Boats. We peeled back one section of a banana, scooped out some of the pulp and filled the cavity with chocolate and marshmallow bits. We put the peel back in place, wrapped the whole thing in tin foil, and baked our stuffed bananas in the coals of our fire. This, I decided, was good! I was sure that we could put this on the menu at Blueberry Hill!

At home, my father slipped in and out. Some adults tried to coax him, "John, you have to eat," they'd say. "Can you sit up? How about one more sip of shake?" "Won't you just take one bite?" To each, he faintly shook his head.

Toward the end of our week, with our elevated cooking skills, our counselors told us we were ready to learn how to make Hay Hole Stew. This, they told us, was a result of having excellent cooking skills, being able to use a knife, being good at direction-following, and, most of all, because we had such enthusiasm. Not every group, they said, learned how to make Hay Hole Stew.

We were excited. As our counselor coached, some of us started to dig a big pit. Some built a fire. Those of us who were the day's cooks peeled carrots, onions, and celery, chopping them up and swirling them in the bottom of a big pot along with cubes of stew beef. We seasoned our stew with just salt and pepper and, after covering it tightly, we lowered the whole steaming pot into the deep hole, which we had completely lined with hay. We weighted the whole thing down with rocks, covered it all with a tarp, and, after putting out our fire, left for the day's excursion.

We hiked for miles that day, all the way to Silver Lake. Singing and swimming, laughing and happy, we spent a blissfully simple day together. Our troop was solid by then. We could cook with the best. And when we got back to camp, we knew, our stew would be ready. And was it! We took off the tarp, moved the rocks, pushed aside the hay, lifted out the pot and found a deliciously fragrant and very tender stew which, with great pleasure and ceremony, we ate.

Hay Hole Stew, we proudly decided, was a grand thing indeed.

And even though it would never get me into "A True Story of Scouts in Action," I couldn't wait to go home and tell my mother about it. Maybe she'd let me make some for the Inn. Maybe she'd let me make some for my father! I knew he'd like it.

But later that afternoon, after we'd packed up camp and had all gone home for the last time, my mother came out to the porch where I was sitting on my little red Mexican chair, shucking corn for the guests' dinner that night. She sat down next to me.

"Daddy is very sick," she said.

I didn't say anything. Why, I wondered, was she telling me this? I picked a few pieces of silk off the corn cobs.

"And, Sweetie Pie," she stopped, "he might die."

Might *die*? I shucked another corn cob, making sure it was perfectly clean. I broke off the end and laid it carefully next to the others for the night's dinner. I picked up another one from the brown paper grocery bag.

"Soon?" I asked, separating a few of the thin tender green husks for her to add to the corn steamer. "A few tender husks added to the corn water makes the corn taste better," my mother'd always said.

"Yes," she answered, "soon."

Again I said nothing. My mother said nothing. I shucked the last ear of corn. Picked up each thread of the corn silk that had fallen on the porch floor. Carried the clean ears into the kitchen. Went out and sat in my maple tree. The sun slipped down over the Adirondacks. Night fell. The evening star came out.

Daddy died that night. Sometime in the middle of the darkness, deep in the middle of an argument with no one, his voice faded and, after a while, stopped. The Inn was very very quiet.

They had moved me and Heather out of Our Room and into Fred's Room, way behind the kitchen, hoping it would be far enough away that we wouldn't hear anything. But late that night we heard loud crying.

I lay in the bed next to Heather, realizing, among other things, that Daddy would never get to try my Hay Hole Stew.

Chapter Twenty

"For Laurey, Who Bakes Fabulous Brownies"

 These days I think they are too sweet, and chocolate tends to give me a headache so I don't even eat it too much, but I was quite the brownie maker (and eater) when I was a kid. I liked them so much that I taught myself to follow a recipe—and became the family brownie maker. I remember the first time I baked. I had learned how to read a couple years before then, but had never tried to follow one of my mother's recipes before.

"You can do it, Pumpkin," my mother had said, busy making dinner for the Inn guests. "Just do what the recipe says."

I opened my mother's first cookbook, *The Blueberry Hill Cookbook*. I was (I can now identify the type) one of those cooks who reads an instruction, does it, then reads the next step, does it, and then moves to the next step. The other method is the one where you get out all the ingredients ahead of time, measure them all and lay them out neatly. This is how the experts do it. That, however, was not my style as an eight-year-old cook.

Sift together twice the flour, baking powder, and salt, my mother's recipe instructed. This involved finding the sifter, climbing up on a stool to reach the counter, measuring all the ingredients into a bowl, finding a piece of waxed paper, spreading it out on the counter, sifting, funneling the ingredients back into the bowl, funneling them into the sifter again (the recipe did say sift twice), doing it all over again, and ending up with as much flour as possible, all nicely sifted, in the mixing bowl.

Over boiling water, combine and melt unsweetened chocolate and butter. Okay, I had to find the double boiler, assemble it, measure the butter, count and unwrap the cubes of chocolate, put them in the double boiler, find matches, light the burner, and try to be patient while the mixture melted. And, no matter how inviting it looked, I had to remember *not* to taste it at this point! Even though it looked delicious, unsweetened chocolate was bitter. A lesson learned the hard way, as they all are, right?

Beat the eggs and gradually add sugar. This meant I had to find the parts for and assemble the mixer, measure the sugar, find the eggs, crack them, pick out the bits of egg shell that inevitably fell into the bowl with the egg, and finally, beat it all together, trying not to spew batter everywhere.

Add chocolate mixture to egg and sugar mixture; beat with electric beater until well blended. Easier said than done on this one. What this really meant was: find the spatula, find a pot holder, scrape the hot chocolate and butter into the mixing bowl. But, after this step it was safe to taste. Yum!

Add flour mixture and blend thoroughly. This step usually created a cloud of flour dust because I often turned the mixer on too high and got flour dust in my nose and all over the counter. Once—well, I think it was just once—I pulled the mixer up out of the mixing bowl before turning it off and splattered little drops of chocolate all over the kitchen. Once was enough to learn that particular lesson! Note to self: do not lift mixer while it is going. Gotcha.

Stir in chopped walnuts and vanilla. Turn the batter into a greased 9-inch square pan. That one was not too hard, except that I had probably forgotten to grease and flour the pan. Another messy step. Should have done it first but I was too busy measuring.

Bake in a moderate oven for 30 or 35 minutes, my mother wrote. *These should not be baked through, but should be slightly moist in the middle when removed from the oven. As they cool, they will firm up quite a bit. If you leave them in the oven long enough to be baked through, they will not have that chewy quality all good brownies should have. Cut into squares while still warm, remove squares from pan, and let cool on a wire rack.*

Now, what this really meant was: you will burn your tongue for certain if you try to eat these before they are cool enough to get out of the pan, so don't! Furthermore, they probably won't even come out of the pan at this point. No matter how much you want to try them, you have to wait.

I became the brownie cooker in my house, keeping us in the gooey dark bars all through my elementary school years. I gradually became less reliant on the recipe, gaining confidence so I could remember what to do and how to do the steps. I still had to look at the recipe for amounts, but I was getting better at the doing of it all.

After my father died, my mother and I moved to Massachusetts, "just for the winter," she'd said. She had closed the Inn for now, it being too much for her to run alone. My mother and I, we had decided, would rent an apartment near my sisters' school and we would all live together, all of us. All of us—that is, in our new, smaller family: me, my mother, and my two sisters.

My mother was very ill too, though I didn't realize it. She slept all the time but I was too young to notice why. Pretty soon, I thought, we'd go back to Vermont. Pretty soon, I would be old enough to cook, and then I would run the Inn. For now I had to go to school in Massachusetts.

In seventh grade, at the Pioneer Valley Regional High School in Massachusetts, all girls had to take either cooking or sewing. Heather and Lucinda, day students at Northfield School for Girls, didn't have to fuss with such stupid things, but I, too young for that private school, was in the local public school.

"We have to take Home Ec!" I sputtered, bounding into my mother's bedroom after the first day at my new school. "They say I have to learn how to *cook!*—unless I can bring a note from home. I don't want to take Home Ec! Yech!" I giggled at my own rhyme. "I want to take shop but girls can't take shop here. Will you please please please write me a note?" I begged, paper and pen conveniently in hand. Obligingly, my mother reached for the pen and paper and wrote a note to the teacher saying I could be excused from this class. "Laurey knows," my mother wrote, "how to cook."

"My mother is Elsie Masterton," I strutted into class the next day, "She wrote the Blueberry Hill cookbooks, and she says I already know how to cook. Here is my note. She says I don't have to take Home Ec." *So there*, I added to myself.

"Well," snapped the teacher, "perhaps you would like to *teach* the class some time! And then you won't have to come anymore. I think it'd be nice for you to show all of us what you know."

I did not like the way she sounded.

"Sure," I scoffed, caught off guard, "*anyone* can teach cooking classes." I knew as I said those words that I was not being very nice. My father would have said, "Don't use that tone of voice with *me*, young lady!" Actually, I was not at all sure I could teach a cooking class, but at that point there was no backing out. I kept going. "My mother even wrote in one of her cookbooks that I bake fabulous brownies! I've watched her do lots of cooking demonstrations." If she could, I could. What was the big deal? I was showing off but could not stop myself. The words poured out. I thought of the many times I'd traveled with my mother, watching her do so many cooking demonstrations that I had grown bored with them and no longer even paid very much attention to what she did. I may have been only twelve and a half years old but I could do it. Of course I could!

"Well, let's have you do a cooking demonstration for us then," the teacher said, an edge in her voice, "I'm sure the class would just love to learn how to make brownies."

Cornered, there was not much I could do except to say I would.

"Class," the teacher said when the day for the demonstration came, "Laurey is going to do a demonstration of how to bake brownies for us, so everyone please pay attention."

Smugly I opened my mother's book and started measuring the ingredients, following my mother's instructions one at a time. The students followed along from the mimeographed sheets I had passed out. I read an instruction. Did the task. Read another instruction. Did the next task. Slowly, very slowly, the ingredients came together. Too slowly. I remembered, just then, that my mother, whenever she had done cooking demonstrations, had always measured out the ingredients ahead of time. Too late for that now, I thought. The class started to fidget. I chewed my cheek, measuring and mixing intently. And then I thought of my mother's demonstrations, remembering how she'd kept up a light bantering with the audience, telling funny stories. I couldn't banter, couldn't think about anything except for the twitching kids who sat gaping at me. This made me even more nervous and made me fear I would miss a step, which slowed me down even more. The boys whispered loudly to each other, griping about when were those brownies going to be done and that they were hungry! They poked at each other, made rude sounds. I hated those kids. My friends in Vermont wouldn't have fidgeted. And in Vermont, I would have taken shop. In Vermont, they'd have known I knew how to cook. Stupid Massachusetts kids, anyway. And where was the teacher? I looked up, saw her standing in the corner of the room, watching me. Why wasn't she making them stop?

When the brownies were finally all mixed up, I put the batter in a pan and put the pan in the oven. Then we waited. And waited. And *then*, all of a sudden but way too late, I remembered my mother putting a pan of batter into the oven in her demonstrations and, at the same time, pulling a finished pan out. Oh, and then, I remembered, there was always the pan that she'd made and baked ahead of time which was all ready to cut and serve. Why oh why had I not done that? By then, the boys were ripping up my recipe sheets and were throwing spit balls at each other. This did not make sense to me. No one threw spit balls during my mother's demonstrations. Why didn't the teacher stop them? And why did I have to even move to Massachusetts? I hated Massachusetts. I wanted to go home to Vermont. I wanted my mother to get out of bed and take me home to Vermont.

That afternoon, when I finally got to leave school, I climbed up to the third floor of the old yellow Victorian house on Highland Avenue. I tiptoed into my mother's room and went to her bed quietly, trying to see if she was asleep. She moved enough to let me know she was awake.

"I made brownies today," I told her.

"And did your friends enjoy them?" she whispered.

"I guess so." It seemed too difficult to tell her all about the boys and the waiting and the teacher and Vermont so I left it at "I guess so."

"That's good, Sweetie," she whispered. "That's good." And once again she drifted off.

Maybe next year, I thought, we would all go back home. And I could bake my fabulous brownies just for my own little family at Blueberry Hill. In Vermont. I could hardly wait.

Laurey's Fabulous Brownies
The Recipe (yum!)

I can't even begin to count the number of these brownies we've made at Laurey's Catering. In the beginning we used a recipe I found in a magazine—a recipe for Katharine Hepburn Brownies. For quite a while we called them that, but then we tweaked the recipe so much that it began to make more sense to just call them our own Brownies. (My mother's brownies were pretty good—but these truly are fabulous!)

So here, finally, for all of you who have asked, is the recipe. To get the best brownies, I suggest you weigh out the ingredients, the way we do.

Makes 24 brownies

The ingredients:

18 ounces unsalted butter (4 ½ sticks)
9 ounces unsweetened chocolate
   (9 squares)
2 pounds plus 1 ounce sugar

9 large eggs
1 teaspoon table salt
4 ½ cups chopped walnuts
6 ounces all-purpose flour

Here's what you do: Preheat a conventional oven to 325°F. Grease and flour a half-size (18 x 13 x 1-inch) commercial sheet pan. You could also use a jelly roll pan, which has almost the same dimensions.

Melt the butter and chocolate in the top of a double boiler.

Using a medium speed, mix the eggs, sugar, and salt with an electric stand mixer, using the paddle attachment. When combined, add the melted butter-chocolate mixture. Add the nuts and flour. When combined, turn to high speed and beat for 45 seconds.

Pour the batter into the prepared pan and bake for 45 minutes or so.

Note: Do not rely on traditional tests for doneness. If you insert a toothpick in them, the toothpick will still be wet. If you wait until it is dry, your brownies will be overcooked. You'll need to pull the brownies out of the oven before they are completely cooked, as they will continue to cook for a bit once they're out and, frankly, moist brownies are so much more enjoyable to eat than dried-up ones, right? When I make them I stop the cooking before the center is completely done, but wait until the edges are fully cooked. The first time you try these I suggest you keep an eye one them. Oh yes, wait until they're cooled before you try to cut them or you could burn your tongue. In my shop we actually chill them overnight and cut them when they are completely cold, though you might not be able to wait that long.

Chapter Twenty-One

Theodore's Parents

 *Theodore lives at 999 Birdfeather Street*, began my favorite childhood book. *His house is always neat, for Theodore looks after everything himself. He cuts the grass and trims the hedge. He fixes the furnace in winter and puts up the awnings in summer.*

I loved this book.

All the mail that comes to 999 Birdfeather Street is for Theodore. When the telephone rings, it is for Theodore. When a salesman knocks at the door and asks, "Is you mother at home?" Theodore says, "I live here and look after everything. What are you selling?"

From the illustrations, it looks like Theodore is about eight or nine in this book. For some reason, when I was little, even after I learned how to read, I asked for it to be read to me over and over and over again.

One day while Theodore was preparing breakfast as usual for himself and Leo (the dog) and Frances (the cat), he said, "I'm starting school today. I'm sorry I must leave you alone. But you can keep each other company and I'll be home by four o'clock.

At school, all the other children tell stories about what they do with their parents, which makes Theodore want some of his own. The book never says why Theodore does not have any parents. He decides to put an ad in the paper:

Wanted: One (1) set of parents. Boy, dog, cat, bird and house provided. Interviews any time next Saturday. At 999 Birdfeather Street.

When the day arrives, Theodore is astonished to find the whole block lined with people, waiting to meet him. He spends the entire day interviewing them, only to find that none of them is what he is looking for.

The next parents were rather nice except that they insisted upon taking Theodore to live with them in a hotel, the book says. *And so it went. Some of the parents were too grouchy and some of them were too sweet. Some of them were too curious and some were not curious enough. None of them would do. After interviewing all day, Theodore sadly told them all "No" and closed the door.*

But then, just as he has decided that he will never find any parents and just after he has started to mix up a batch of muffins, the doorbell rings. When Theodore opens the door, he sees a man, a woman, and a little girl standing in front of him, apologetic to be so late, but asking if the parent position is still available.

The position, Theodore tells them, *is* still available. Theodore interviews them and the next day they move in and take him and his new little sister to the zoo, after they eat the muffins that Theodore's new mother has just baked.

"You girls need to come to Vermont tonight," the person on the phone said to Lucinda one afternoon in late October. "Your mother is, well, she is, um, well you all three just need to come to Vermont as soon as you can."

Lucinda was sixteen. Heather was fourteen. I was just twelve. My sisters were trying to be good students, but it was hard. About two weeks before that phone call, someone had come and taken my mother off to the hospital near us. But then someone else decided to take her back up to Vermont, to the doctors who knew her medical history. Somehow, after that phone call on that afternoon in October, we all managed to get to Vermont. Lucinda must have driven the three of us on the four-hour ride that day.

When we got to the hospital, a nurse met us and took us to the room. This hospital did not have any lines painted on the floor. I wondered for a moment about little packets of jelly and toast, but that thought disappeared as soon as we got next to my mother's bed.

My two sisters and I just stood and looked at her.

A few minutes after the nurse had let us into my mother's room, she ushered us out again. "Your mother is very tired," she said. "But," she continued, cheerfully, "I can tell she's glad to see you. She's glad you came!"

I couldn't see how anyone could know anything about what my mother might have been thinking. The person in that bed did not look like my mother, and I, for one, could not understand any of the sounds she was making.

"Okay, girls," someone said, "you can come back tomorrow. Right now the Blairs are waiting at their house for you. You'd better get going."

I guess things would be different now, but then, even though we'd driven for all that time, and even though we'd only stayed for five minutes, and even though she was as sick as she was, they made us leave. Heather and I were there against the rules anyway: "Visitors to patient rooms must be 16 and older" the sign at the reception desk said. But someone had snuck us in, though we'd probably have just gone in anyway, even if someone had tried to stop us.

We drove to Middlebury, arriving at the Blairs' home under a dark fall sky after another hour in the car. The Blairs, friends of our parents, had agreed to take us in for the night.

"Come in, girls," Mrs. Blair said. The Blair's daughter Suzy was a friend of ours and for some reason, at that point, that house was the only place we could go. No one had arranged anything else.

"You're just in time. Dinner is ready," she said.

We were not hungry. And we had nothing to say. We all sat in the Blairs' dining room. The Blairs ate and tried to start conversations, but none of us answered. And none of us ate anything.

Out in the vestibule the phone rang.

Mr. Blair got up from the table to answer it. We heard his voice murmuring, heard him hang up the phone, and watched him come back into the dining room, his eyes following a pattern on the edge of the Oriental carpet. He looked at Mrs. Blair, but he didn't say anything.

For some reason we all stood up, went out into the hallway, got in a circle and hugged each other. All of us. The Blairs and me and my two sisters just stood and hugged. No one spoke. No one cried. But we all, somehow, knew this is what we should do.

We stayed with the Blairs until the day after the funeral was over. The whole thing was strange. I wore the same jumper someone had bought for me for Daddy's funeral, just three months before. I had not worn it at all since then, and it still itched. Once again I was the only one not dressed in black. Whoever had bought that jumper did not buy black. I felt strange, being the only one in orange plaid.

We went back to the same funeral home, rode in the same limousine, went to the Brandon Inn after the graveside service, and picked at the same grey turkey slices until it was time to leave.

But this time we didn't know where to go. We did not have anyone to live with. Until someone could help us figure it out, my sisters and I drove back to the apartment in Massachusetts and tried to live a normal life. About once a week my uncle would call with a suggestion of what we could do, but his ideas were always awful and so we just stayed put.

Every once in a while someone would show up with some cookies, but, for the most part, we took care of ourselves for three months. In a way, it seemed normal.

I mean, Theodore had done it.

We had a routine. Every Wednesday night we'd drive to Greenfield, the next big town over, to do the laundry. While the clothes were in the washing machines, we'd go to the Friendly's restaurant next door and order cheeseburgers on grilled bread, which seemed so very exotic to me. Grilled bread! Wow! We'd go back to the Laundromat and shift our clothes to the dryers and then, during the drying cycles, we'd go to a movie. We three divided up the chores at home, cooking and cleaning and doing our homework. We thought we were doing just fine. But a neighbor complained and so our uncle told us we had to find someone to live with.

I remembered *Theodore's Parents.*

"Let's put an ad in the newspaper!" I suggested, kind of excited by the idea. It had worked for Theodore, after all.

Lucinda and Heather didn't like the idea of an ad but they both knew the book too, and together we decided to invite possible candidates, one at a time, to visit for a weekend. There had been a short list of people who had offered to help out, "if anything happened to you and John, Elsie." We'd called all these people and they all told us that they'd only meant that they'd be willing to take *one* of us. And that, we all agreed, was not an option.

It wasn't a whole lot different from Theodore's experience before his parents finally arrived. We met a whole bunch of odd, unacceptable people. One woman took one look at the three sets of stairs leading up to our third floor apartment and left immediately. One woman started yelling at us as soon as we picked her up at the train station, scolding us about how she didn't think we were wearing enough clothes. We all looked at each other and took her back to the train before she could even get out of the car. We did not, however, have a line of candidates strung out down the block, and in our story, no one showed up after all the other interviews were done, though I kept listening for the doorbell all night. I kept waiting for the muffins.

Finally one of us remembered Liz Allen. Liz had worked with my mother at the Inn and, when our parents got sick, my mother had asked Liz if she'd look out for us "if anything bad happened." Well, bad things had happened. So we called her and, after talking it over with her husband, she agreed to let us move into an apartment in New York City with them and their young son.

We lived with the Allens for one year until it just became too difficult for all of us. Three teenagers is quite a handful, especially after they have lived alone for three months, and finally we all decided that it just was not going to work anymore. Heather and I, it was decided by my uncle and the psychiatrist he hired, would go to boarding school and Lucinda would finish up her last three months of her senior year of high school living in the city, with yet another family. Much against our protests, we were split up.

And I guess all I can say is that we made it through, but for a very long time I felt like the whole thing was very unfair. It should have happened to us the same way it happened to Theodore, I thought. It was, after all, what I had read in that book.

From *Theodore's Parents*, by Janice May Udry, 1958, Lothrop, Lee & Shepard.

Chapter Twenty-Two

Maple Syrup

 It is syruping time in Vermont again. Happens every March or, that is, whenever the spring thaws come. Warm days and cold nights make the sap run. Makes things perfect for syruping.

The spring of my thirteenth year, after we left Blueberry Hill for good and were living with the Allens in New York City, we took a trip to Vermont and I tapped and made maple syrup for the first time.

One of the big maples across the road from the Inn already had a tap in its trunk. There were actually three maples there, all in a row. One summer, a few years earlier, Lucinda and Heather and I had all built tree houses in those trees. Well, we had only used two of the three trees. Lucinda and Heather had claimed the one at the far end of the row, the one which hung over the sand bank above the Beaver Dam Road where Heather and I often played at making campfires and pretending to cook things. I chose the tree nearest the Inn because it had the lowest branches and I had hammered a couple of boards into its trunk a couple of weeks before and had dragged some more boards up into the branches, already starting on my treehouse. It surprised me, that day, that Lucinda and Heather were even playing with me, since they usually were too busy with their own projects to spend time with me. But I was happy to be out there with them and was only a little disappointed that they were building a house together and I was building one alone.

Theirs was an entire complex! Lucinda was the most artistic one of the three of us, after all. She designed our dollhouse furniture, sewed, painted, and drew. Heather, not so artistic, was a very good follower and did whatever Lucinda suggested. The treehouse grew quickly with their combined skills. Mine was really just a patchwork of boards nailed into the closest branch, about as good as an eight-year-old could do.

For some reason, in choosing our treehouse trees, we skipped that one tree in the middle. Maybe its branches were too high or there weren't enough of them, or maybe the tree was just too tall and thin. An old pipe, jammed into the trunk during a maple syrup season years ago, poked out of the trunk. Could sap have ever come from that gaunt scrap of a tree? That day, in building our houses, we ignored the middle tree, playing in our other two perches, stringing our telephone can system around the thin, small tree in between.

It was March, that year we went back to Vermont with the Allens. That very first year, needing to close up the Inn, we all drove to Vermont during our spring vacation: Liz and Claude, Matthew their two-year-old, their new baby Sarah, and the three of us.

At the Inn, Liz and my sisters puttered around my mother's kitchen, packing and sorting. Bored, I wandered across the road to the bank with those three maples, exploring and remembering my old secret places. My sisters' treehouse still stood, sturdy as it had been when they'd built it four years before. Mine remained too, still crooked, and still very much my creation. A shredded American flag fluttered from my treehouse porch.

A tiny movement caught my eye—a single drop of clear liquid, collected on the tap of that scrawny middle maple tree, dripped off the edge of the pipe. I walked closer and saw a stream of sap dripping from that old pipe, flowing out, strong and steady. I flew to the barn, found an old bucket, ran back to the tree, hung it up, and started collecting that sap. My timing was perfect. The weather, just right, made the sap pour out of the tap. My small bucket filled to the brim four or five times during that one afternoon. I collected every drop I could.

Later, when it grew dark, I poured my sap into a big pot and started to boil it down, right there in the kitchen of Blueberry Hill, right there in my mother's kitchen. Right on my mother's stove, I put it on to boil.

Now, a Vermont child learns about maple syrup in school. Each year, in the middle of sugaring season, our neighbors celebrated with "sugar-on-snow" parties. Sap boiled and boiled until it became thick and then, at just the right time, when a candy thermometer instructed, the mess all got poured onto a bowlful of clean snow. The hot caramel hardened instantly, becoming sticky, way-too-sweet taffy. Vermonters ate the taffy with bland donuts and tart pickles—an odd combination to be sure, but that's what they did. "Sugar-on-snow" parties, a once-a-year tradition, were the signal that winter was almost gone and spring was well on the way. Cold nights. Warm days. Sap ran, boiled hour after hour over fires tended in sheds out in the woods, thickening into rich, pure syrup.

But that spring afternoon there was not enough time to boil my four buckets of sap into syrup. It takes a lot of sap, gallons, to make just one quart of syrup. And it takes hours and hours to boil. Hours and hours. I didn't start my boiling until Sunday afternoon. There was not enough time. We had to leave, Liz said. We had to leave our real home to go back to the apartment in New York City.

I took my sap with me, my gallons of partly-made syrup. I guarded the jars, my precious jars of sap, in the back seat of the car all the way back to the city. My sap had become a little bit thicker, just a little bit thicker from its one short hour of boiling. I carried my jars from Vermont up in the elevator and brought them down the hall to Apartment 5G, our apartment in New York City in that ugly white building on the corner of Eighty-sixth Street and First Avenue.

And in that little apartment kitchen I finished my boiling, a day or two of intermittent cooking, this time in one of Liz's spaghetti sauce pots. I made a moist mess, sticky sap evaporating in that tiny kitchen, sweet in the air, collecting in teardrops on the walls, steaming up the windows. Boiling and thickening. My Blueberry Hill sap. My—by then—single cup of beautiful, deep amber maple syrup. Elixir of the gods. Heaven. Vermont. Home. My trees, my heart, my everything boiled down in that small pan.

I poured my syrup into a mason jar, capped it, and stowed it in the refrigerator door next to Liz's margarine and Claude's Martini olives. I rationed myself. A fingerful was all I allowed myself at one time, two dips of a finger a day at the very most. But even at that rate I knew my one cup of syrup would not last nearly long enough.

No one else was allowed to have *any* of it. I let no one have one bit. Not even a taste. No. Not any one of them. I checked in on my jar of syrup every day that spring and into the early part of the summer, unscrewing the cap, dipping my finger, and tasting my real home, my bit of my Vermont home in the refrigerator door of that New York apartment.

It was almost more than I could bear—this jar of my life.

It finally had to be thrown out. It got a green mold. I had not eaten it fast enough. And I still would not let anyone go near it. I couldn't bear the thought that it might be gone. And then one day it finally rotted. One day, one awful day, my whole jar disappeared. Liz Allen, I realized, had poured it down the sink.

It is spring again and the sap is probably starting to run in Vermont. It stirs me now as it does every year at this time. As it does with each taste of maple syrup. Every time. Always has, and probably always will.

Chapter Twenty-Three

Miss Beard's School for Young Ladies

"Your mother ate here when she was a little girl," Uncle Sidney, my mother's oldest brother, said from across the dark paneled booth. Heather and I sat, politely nodding and picking at our hot fudge sundaes. "She always ordered a Hot Fudge Sundae, and always got two cherries." Heather and I didn't say anything. To tell you the truth, we felt like we were being sent to prison.

Back when we still lived at the Inn, we begged our mother to tell us stories. "Tell the one about when you used to stand in your front yard crying," we'd coax, listening as she told about when she was just three, and would lure innocent pedestrians who, at her insistence that she was lost, would take her to the police station just down the street where she would get an ice cream cone and an escort back to her front yard. Sitting there at Grunig's, I remembered many nights at the Inn when my mother calmed herself after the dinner rush by sitting in front of the fire in the den, savoring a bowl of Maple Walnut Ice Cream with a drizzle of Maple Syrup.

And there I was, with my uncle, sitting where my mother had sat many years before. Ice cream, I was seeing, had quite a history with her.

Heather and I were sitting with Uncle Sidney, full of dread about our next home. Well, I was pretty sure it would not be home, but it was where we were going to live for a while, at least during the school year.

The whole situation with the Allens had blown up, which was not really such a surprise. Three strong-headed girls were really too much for a young couple with two small children. And no one listened when we said we wanted to run the Inn. How could teenagers run an Inn anyway? Boarding school, announced Uncle Sid, was the answer. And now he was trying to ease us into the move, which was not working very well. I remember fuming, livid at the fact that Lucinda, who only had three months left of her senior year of high school, was going to stay in New York. No matter how much we had protested and pleaded to be kept together, we were now being split up. Lucinda was staying in New York. Heather and I were sent off to boarding school in New Jersey.

"It's so close, you'll be able to visit each other all the time," Uncle Sid had said. It had not seemed to matter to him that we did not want to leave Vermont. It had not seemed to matter that we had not wanted to go to New York. Nor had he listened when we had implored him to let us stay together. "It's only a short bus ride away."

Uncle Sid thought ice cream, at our mother's favorite ice cream parlor, would help. The ice cream was good, but he was wrong. It did not help. And, about where we going to live there was not much that we could do. Three girls, aged fourteen, sixteen, and eighteen. The adults were making the decisions. Ice cream was not going to fix anything.

"Attention girls," a voice came from the head of the dining room that night, "I'd like you all to welcome our two newest boarders, Heather and Laurey. Make them welcome. Now bow your heads for the blessing." And off she went, droning on in a monotone about "God" and "this food" and "Amen."

Everyone droned "Amen," and then, chairs scraping, sat.

At my table, Ginny, a gawky girl with buck teeth and very skinny legs that stuck out from her old-fashioned looking green wool pinafore, grinned at me, got up, went to the kitchen, and came back with bowls of really awful looking food. One oval dish held something green. A closer look, which I got as the bowl came to me, revealed spinach, straight from a can, nasty and tangled and looking not much different than weeds might have looked. I passed the bowl on.

"You must at least *try* everything," barked the woman at the head of my table. "You may call me Miss Howland," she added. I looked around for Heather. She seemed happy, sitting at another table and already telling stories to a rapt audience.

I took the bowl, put a small serving on my plate and passed it on. Ginny, sitting next to me, poked me in the leg. Startled, I looked at her.

"Watch me," she hissed, "I'll show you what to do."

A platter of meatloaf came to me. Meatloaf with—could this be—an egg in it? Yes, each slice of meatloaf, which I'd always hated anyway, had a thick slice of hard-boiled egg in the middle of it, a greenish tinge ringing the yolk. Wanting to pass the platter without taking any, I glanced to the head of the table, saw the glare, took the smallest piece, and passed it on. I thought back to the afternoon, wishing I was back at Grunig's, wishing I was anywhere but at this table. The last bowl contained mashed potatoes. I took a small spoonful and passed it on.

When all the bowls had completed the circuit of the table, Miss Howland announced, "You may begin."

Ginny, at my side, poked me again. I watched as she pretended to eat, all the while keeping an eye on Miss Howland. When Miss Howland looked down, Ginny flipped a forkful of spinach into her lap, catching it in her napkin. She glanced at me, grinned a crooked grin, and ate her mashed potatoes. Ginny was a master. (One time, later in the year, I watched as she tucked green beans into her cheek, ate everything else on her plate—well, everything that she hadn't flipped into her lap—and then, back in her room after dinner, spit out the beans into her garbage can. She was amazing!)

The cooking at the Beard School was just plain awful. Brought over from Poland, the cooks probably tried their best, but the ingredients were not good, mostly cans of vegetables served from a steam table. I could hear my mother's voice in my head every time I went by the steam table. My mother hated steam tables, refused to have one at Blueberry Hill, and sneered at anyone who had one anywhere else. If she suspected a restaurant might have one, she'd choose someplace else. Steam table food, synonymous with "awful," was to be avoided at all costs. At the Beard School, everything was served from a steam table.

Fortunately, we in the boarding department came up with strategies to compensate. Ann Spitz, the other boarder in my class of just nine girls, provided a constant source of junk food, supplied for the most part by her father. "Guilt food," we called it. She wrote him sad letters and he would come to visit, take her out to dinner, and send her back with bags full of snacks. She brought M+Ms by the pound bag full, Cheese Balls by the can, and Droste Chocolate Apples that broke into wedges when you cracked them on a table. She brought bags of Jolly Roger hard candies, salted peanuts in the shell, Cracker Jack, Pepperidge Farm cookies, and Swiss chocolate bars. When she came back from a "guilt food" outing we would sit in her room and eat until we were completely stuffed, queasy from it all. No matter how much we ate, there was always more for the next day.

We also figured out how to sneak off the small block "island" that was the Beard School campus. Younger girls were not allowed to leave the block, but that did not stop us. Rather, it made the journey all the more inviting and irresistible. The soda shop on the corner of Scotland Avenue made great chocolate ice cream sodas and that was enough of a reason to chance getting caught. We bought cakes, pies, cookies, and gooey desserts, sneaking them back to our rooms for late night feasts. We'd tuck them into our underwear drawers, knowing that they were safe until after dinner, when we'd go up and, in between games of jacks, cram handfuls of strawberries and whipped cream in our mouths, laughing until we choked. What were they going to do to us anyway, make us go without dinner? We hoped!

Occasionally someone would invite us for an off-campus outing. Laurie Lazar's parents took us to one of the most extravagant buffets I've ever seen, even now, with one whole room filled with displays of raw clams and snow crab legs and smoked oysters. There were huge carving boards with roast beef and ham and turkey. One room held towers of shrimp cocktail, bowls and bowls of olives of all kinds and bright salads, breads, soups, strawberries with chocolate for dipping and on and on and then, when we were quite full, a whole separate dessert room beckoned. Full of pastries and tiny little éclairs and powdery puffs of sugar confections that sent me into a sweet spin, I was delirious. My mother would have *loved* it!

There were other dining out experiences. Once two of our teachers took me and my friend Jody to a fancy restaurant where we had duck á l'orange and cherries jubilee which the waiter flambéed at the side of our table, making us feel very adult. One time my friend Ditto's father took us to Palisades Amusement Park, letting us ride on all the rides, play all the games of chance, and buy anything and everything we wanted to eat: hot dogs, cotton candy, caramel apples, salty peanuts in the shell, coke, sausage and onions rolls, funnel cakes, snow cones and chocolate dipped frozen bananas. No wonder the rides became less appealing as the day went on!

But truthfully, the very best was when, after a day's outing of bowling or going to a movie, a group of us boarders ended up back at Grunig's where I always ordered a California Burger (which came with lettuce and tomato—how radical!). For dessert, I always got a Hot Fudge Sundae. "My mother used to eat here when she was a little girl," I'd say every time, wondering if she had sat in this very booth. Who knows, I'd think to myself, maybe she had. And that, for a moment, made me feel better.

Chapter Twenty-Four

Bagels

 At Miss Beard's School for Young Ladies, all boarding students had to choose a place of worship on Sunday. It was a requirement, just like walking around the block each morning before school. "Young ladies need exercise," intoned Miss Howland. "You will walk around the block each morning."

"Then why," we demanded, "can't we walk around the block in the afternoon?"

Miss Howland's face turned red and she stomped off, her pedometer clicking against her fat legs. We thought we heard something about "kids" and "insolence" and "no *wonder* their parents sent them away" before she turned the corner to her frigid office.

"All girls attend a church of their own choosing," Miss Sutherland announced to me and Heather in our first week at the Beard School for Young Ladies. "You may try out a few to see which you like, but you must attend some place."

All of this was new to us. I'd been to church with Miss Moore when I was really little, and even had my name printed on a box of envelopes one year. Miss Moore gave me a nickel to put in my envelope, and showed me how to put it in the collection plate at the tiny First Episcopal Church of Forest Dale.

I choose the Presbyterians at first. My best friend Foncee went to that church and I liked being where she was. She generally followed boys, like a shark after a school of sardines. I didn't care about the boys, but I did like Foncee and I especially liked the cookies that the Presbyterians served as soon as the service finished. We didn't have to go back to school until after the whole service finished, which, to me, included cookie hour. Not to mention that no one minded how many cookies we ate. I played lacrosse at the Beard School for Young Ladies, and I could eat a lot of cookies. My school uniform had pockets too, so there was plenty of room to stash the handfuls of Milanos, Oreos, and Pecan Sandies that didn't fit into my stomach.

Foncee eventually drifted over to the Episcopalians. No doubt a cute boy had popped onto her screen. Wendy Lawrence, a regular Episcopalian, must have told her. Foncee, a Cherokee from the middle of Ohio, was *not* an Episcopalian, but boys were boys and so she made the shift. I followed right behind.

But the Episcopalians did not have good food. They really didn't have any food except for the communion wine and wafer and I just did not feel right about going up to the front to get any of this. The Presbyterians had communion, but they brought a little tray of individual cups of grape juice and another tray of little bread cubes and no one watched as we took a couple of each in the safety of our pew. But at the Episcopal church, you had to get up, walk up past all those real Episcopal people, kneel down in front of everyone, and say some words. I didn't know what the words were and I also didn't like kneeling in front of a whole church full of people. Plus, they said things that I didn't really believe in or understand, so I figured I'd better try to do something different.

"My synagogue serves bagels and lox, or rather, Nova, on Sundays," Sue, a girl in my class, cooed. "Plus it is our year to study Comparative Religion so we are visiting all kinds of other churches. *And*," she added, not that I cared, "there are boys!"

Sue was one of those not-very-popular girls who, for some reason, really liked me. I had related the stories about the Presbyterians and their cookies and Episcopalians and my communion dilemma to her, which made her leap at the chance to have more time with me. I did not want more time with her and I did not care about the boys either, but the idea of bagels was interesting. Any food was interesting.

"What *is* a bagel, anyway?" I'd asked.

"You're kidding me!" she howled, "How can you not know what a bagel is?"

"Or, um, Nova?" I dared confess further.

"You *have* led a sheltered existence up there in Vermont, haven't you?" she blurted.

This was not making me like her any more, but I put up with her as she explained. Bagels. Hot bagels, she had said. And Nova, thin and pink and salty. This was worth exploring.

The switch was easy. She was right. Mr. Levine, the Sunday school teacher, drove into the town of Orange each Sunday before school, picked up right-out-of-the-oven bagels, a tub of scallion cream cheese, and a white paper packet filled with layers and layers of translucent slices of the most delicate, salty, pale-orange salmon I'd ever seen.

"You slice the bagel, so," Mr. Levine instructed, "and do *not* cut your hand! Spread on some cream cheese, just a *schmear*, and then take your fork like this," he lifted a slice, "and lay it on the cream cheese. Voilà! That's bagels and lox, I mean, Nova!"

I tried it, slicing the bagel that was still hot, spreading on the cream cheese, flaking on a couple of slices of salmon, squishing them around with my fork. I bit in. Cream cheese squished out around the sides of the bagel. Oh my! The chilly salmon, the hot bagel, the cream cheese. This, I knew in a flash, beat *every* other possible option for Sundays.

Wow! What a way to start a day!

I learned a lot about other religions that year. The Baptists could sing. The Quakers were very quiet. The Bahai had a beautiful building but seemed oddly distant. But there was nothing to lure me away since no one else had very good food. Bagels. Why go anywhere else?

Chapter Twenty-Five

Cornish Game Hens for Dinner

 It took some time and practice before I could manage the challenge of putting a whole meal together at one time. I don't have to stop and think about what and how and when to do what anymore, and in fact I can put whole meals together for hundreds of people—often without a kitchen, but in my early days there were some memorable crashes.

The first whole meal I tried to cook was when I was still in high school, living with my sister Lucinda and her husband Ed. Miss Beard's School for Young Ladies had fallen apart, to no one's surprise. Too many girls realized that there was more to life than sneaking off campus to buy cake, and they were able to convince their parents to send them somewhere else. Heather graduated, which left just me and one other girl in the dorm. The school decided to merge with a boy's school. The boarding department, after June, was finished.

On the day in February that my sister Lucinda got married I sat at the bar of the little hotel in Evanston, Illinois with her and asked her if I could live with her. I think she was about ready to walk down the aisle or I might have I asked her right after the wedding was done. I was sixteen and couldn't figure out what else to do.

She said yes. What else was there to say? She and her husband lived with each other for a few months and then, as soon as summer was over, I moved in with them.

Lucinda and I shared cooking and cleaning responsibilities. The cook was excused from dish duty. I washed a lot of dishes, because Lucinda cooked much better than I did. She did, however, have a unique talent for being able to use every single pot, spoon, and dish in the house, but I put up with that since she made such delicious meals. My repertoire was mostly a once-a-week pot of chili which lasted for two nights. I cooked in one pot. She had one pot, three bowls, and three spoons to wash. Dishes on my cooking nights took about three minutes. Lucinda cooked Chicken à l'Orange, Swedish Meatballs, Smothered Steaks. She used up all the pots and all the pans. We ate with pleasure, but I washed a whole lot of dishes.

One week Lucinda went away, leaving Ed—my new brother-in-law—and me to fend for ourselves for a few days. We ate pizza one night, went out for hamburgers one night and then, once I'd screwed up enough courage, I decided to cook. Ed invited his friend Phidge to come to our house at seven. I planned and thought and read and went through all the steps in my head, wanting to make a good dinner and feeling that I needed to make a good impression on Ed's friend. The reality was that Ed and his friend would have been perfectly content with hamburgers or another trip to the pizza spot, but I would have none of that.

This was my big chance.

I decided to make Cornish Game Hens, a Rice Pilaf (really Rice-A-Roni), and Green Beans. (It amazes me to think that this meal could possibly involve any fear or concern on my part, but it did.) I decided to have Tapioca Pudding for dessert.

I planned and worried and thought about my meal for the entire day. Here I was, finally cooking for guests! I'd watched my mother do this. And I was Elsie Masterton's daughter, after all, so if she could do it, I could, too. I was nervously sure I could do it.

I started getting ready early in the afternoon, carefully figuring out how long everything would take to cook, planning when I would put all the different parts into the oven or onto the stove, imagining how I would set the table.

First of all, I cleaned the hens, seasoned them, and put them in the oven just as my reference book, *Joy of Cooking*, instructed. They seemed kind of frozen still, even though I'd taken them out of the freezer an hour or so earlier, so I put them into the oven a little bit early. Thinking I was giving the hens plenty of time to cook, I backed up the cooking time for the rice and the green beans. I fussed with the oven, getting the roasting pan situated just right. It was very important to me that everything come out at just the right time. I had heard my mother snipping about those poor people who could not manage this simple task. I did not want the same thing to happen to me.

And, while I was still worried about time, I guessed the rice would stay warm for a while and I would be able to set it on the back of the stove if got done too early, so I cooked it too and then checked on the hens, which, through the oven door, did not seem too far from being done. The vegetables, a package of frozen green beans, sat in an icy block, unwrapped and ready in a steamer on the back burner of our stove.

I set the table. This was going just fine! I was doing it! I was managing a whole meal.

Everything seemed to be going well and, just as Phidge arrived, I turned up the heat under the beans. It looked like the rice was just about done, as were the hens, it appeared. Everything would be ready in the time it took to cook the beans, I figured. I *had* watched my mother do this, watched her gracefully turning knobs and stirring pots and poking into ovens full of roasts and such. For her it seemed like a dance. I had only these three items on my menu. What was the big deal?

Just as the beans finished cooking, the guys announced they were ready to eat.

I put the food onto our three plates, stalling as long as I possibly could, because the hens, once I poked them with a fork, did not seem to be quite finished. Actually, they seemed a bit, well, frozen still. I put a mound of rice, a hen (hoping that my fork test was wrong) and a spoonful of green beans on each plate. I even drizzled a bit of browned butter on the beans. This was way before I had any awareness of "plate presentation" but the food looked good to me.

I had done it! Ta da!!!

As nervous as I was, I couldn't eat, but held my fork in my hand, watching to see how my dinner would be received. I nervously stared as Phidge took the first bite of rice. I watched him lift the fork to his mouth, and then heard—a crunch! Oh no! The rice was not done. I was *sure* I'd given it enough time. I looked down at my plate, set down my fork. I felt my face heating up. Meanwhile Ed cut into his game hen and I saw that, even though the outside of the hen looked brown, the inside was—yes—still a chunk of ice. Why hadn't I just ordered pizza? Phidge put his fork down. Ed too. I remember wishing I could melt away, turn invisible. I felt awful. This, to me, was a tremendous humiliation, a dishonoring of my heritage, a mark against me (not that anyone else was keeping track!).

With tremendous embarrassment I took our plates off the table, put the hens back in the oven, scraped the rice back into the pan on the stove. We ate the green beans.

A half hour later we ate the rice, which was singed and sticky and unappetizingly clumpy. And then, probably an hour later, after I checked again and again and finally found them done, we ate the hens. I felt so horrible. I called my sister, crying and terribly upset that I had made such a horrible mess of this momentous occasion. She chuckled, soothed me, and suggested that the guys had certainly forgotten the whole meal the minute it was done. She suggested we eat the pudding, which we did.

And then I, alone, washed the dishes.

Chapter Twenty-Six

Finest Kind

 My friend Carolyn got me a great start in food. She didn't know it, nor did I at the time, but, wanting to take a break from my college studies, and looking for something other than the dark of a theatre's backstage, where I had been finding myself more and more, I spent one summer on Cape Cod. I tried to fish but quickly discovered a propensity for seasickness. Not a good thing, since commercial fishing trips generally last for a few days and once out, there is no turning back. On my last fishing trip the water was so rough and I was so scared that I promised myself that if I made it back to land, I'd quit the foolishness of commercial fishing and stay on land, safe and dry.

"Say, Laurey," it was Carolyn again on the phone, calling a week after my ill-fated fishing expedition. "I got you another job! Finest kind!"

"Right," I responded warily. "Finest kind," on the Cape, meant something top-notch. But she'd said the same thing about my spot on the fishing boat. And that was definitely *not* "finest kind."

"And what might that be?"

"Stripping nets!" she chirped.

"And, um, what's stripping nets?" I asked.

"Oh, it's easy. You go over to Wacky Jack's house. You take an old fishing net, one that's all knotted up and not usable anymore. You take a knife and you cut the knotted net off the lines that it is tied to. And then Janice, Jack's wife, will tie a new net on. Best part is, it's on land! You'll love it!"

"Sure," I replied, not at all convinced.

But in actuality, it was not a bad job. Feet firmly planted on a newly paved cul-de-sac in the middle of a not-quite-developed residential neighborhood, I stripped nets, earning ten dollars a net. And since I didn't need much money, I felt no compulsion to do more than three or four nets on any given day, a couple of times each week. After all, my friend Jill and I had paid for the whole summer's rental on the cottage we lived in, so there was none of that to worry about. And many of our friends worked fishing or clamming or crabbing so there was never a shortage of things to eat.

For amusement, Carolyn and I had figured out the trick to the pinball machine at the local bar so that, for an investment of one quarter and one beer, we could drink and play pinball for the whole night for free. Here's what we did: We knew that, without too much difficulty, the second person to use this one specific pinball machine could win the game, so each night we teamed up, bought ourselves a drink apiece, and started playing a game on that machine. If someone wanted to play the winner of any of the bar games—pool, pinball, or air hockey—they put a quarter on the machine and waited to play the winner of the current game. Of course if Carolyn and I played each other, one of us had to win and then the person waiting his turn would play the winner of our match. We, being gracious, would let the unknowing challenger go first. And then, knowing that the second person could easily win on this machine, we'd beat him. Likewise, the next player, and the next. We played for drinks, the loser buying us a drink of our choice. And then we'd go on to play the next person in line. We had our drinks well taken care of for that whole summer.

But back to the eating. Carolyn's friend Tut was a great fisherman, always showing up and saying, "C'mon, let's go catch some king mackerel!" or "Who wants to go crabbing?" "Anyone want to get some lobster?" I always jumped at the chance.

Tut knew the schedule of the shellfish wardens, and could keep us out of trouble (though we finally just bought a license, which meant we could follow the rules and dig or catch our fill each day). When it came to digging steamers or looking for razor clams, Tut was our man. And while he was not much of a cook, more like a grizzled fisherman who drank too much, he liked me and told me how the local people prepared the local fish.

"You take a bluefish," he'd say, "and you lay it on a tray. You cut up a red onion and a tomato and you lay them on the fish. And then you smear mayonnaise on the whole thing. And you broil it. Just what the 'Portagee' do."

Tut taught me lots of Portuguese cooking that summer.

"Finest kind," he'd say, sampling my concoctions, "finest kind."

I spent a lot of time reading cookbooks, pouring over the *New York Times* Sunday magazine, tearing out the recipe pages, starting to do real cooking. One recipe looked really good: a recipe by Craig Claiborne and Pierre Franey for Baked Stuffed Quahogs.

"You say CO-hogs," Tut said, "or else they'll *know* you're an off-Cape ignoramus. Do *not* let me catch you saying quay-hog or qua-hog. It's CO-hog, got me?"

"CO-hog," I practiced.

"Yup, see this little bit of purple on the shell? That was the original wampum back in the days of the Mayflower."

Tut knew a little bit about everything.

"Maybe you should make some of those clams for Fourth of July, for Carolyn's party," he continued. "Wolfe can get you the clams."

"Yup, he's right," Carolyn agreed. "I'm having a party all right. It's a tradition. Tons of people come. Baked Stuffed Quahogs would be great. I could eat about twenty right this very second!"

Carolyn, short and round, loved eating. Loved my cooking. Encouraged me whenever she could. "Yeah—let's have you make those for the party. I'll tell Wolfie to dig up some clams for you."

There were two days until July 4th. I studied the recipe: fresh clams, bacon, onions, celery, fresh dill, Parmesan cheese, butter, white wine. Seemed easy enough, though I would need to get to the grocery store.

I spent the next day stripping nets. I did five, I think, knowing that the ingredients, the ones other than the clams, were going to be pricey. Carolyn wanted me to make "a ton."

"This crowd can *eat!*" she said.

I was fidgety all day, jumpy all night, anxious to get started with this big cooking project. Would they like them? Could I do them? Cooking for a crowd? Wow!

On the morning of July 4th, Wolfe, true to Carolyn's word, showed up with three huge bushel bags bursting with softball-size clams. These clams were big enough to become soup bowls, for crying out loud, I thought. His bags bulged.

"I got 150 pounds for you," he crowed. A hundred and fifty pounds of clams! Holy Mazoly!

I got busy.

Carolyn had a rigged-up quahog opener her father had made a long time ago that she dragged out for the occasion. It was actually an old knife with a hole drilled in the tip of the blade. A pin went through the hole and attached to a frame so that the knife could pivot up and down, and could come down with a good amount of force on a clamshell's seam, slicing through it like it was a lemon. This sure beat opening each clam with a clam knife, especially since these clams were so big. Carolyn clamped the quahog opener to a table out in her yard and started opening.

The recipe called for grinding the clams with the onions, the bacon, the herbs. The mixture then was spooned back into the shells, sprinkled with wine and Parmesan, and broiled. Our little cottage's kitchen had a grinder, fortunately, and a huge bowl. And, for some reason, lots of trays.

We set up a production line: Carolyn opened the clams, I ground them, seasoned them, spooned them into the empty shell halves. We laid them out on cookie sheets and filled the refrigerator with them, stacking the shelves, tray upon tray upon tray. Carolyn blasted the Allman Brothers, and we kept ourselves well "beveraged," to say the least. This was going to be some party! Friends started to appear, carrying beer, chips, fried clams, blue crabs, oysters, corn for roasting, cheese dips, macaroni and potato salads, layered puddings, pies, cakes, and homemade ice cream.

As the middle of the afternoon rolled around, I started cooking the clams. I baked a tray for about five minutes and then, right at the end, I stuck them under the broiler, tray after tray after tray. Carolyn carried them out to the lawn. And tray after tray after got eaten.

"Make more!" Carolyn's friends shouted.

And I did.

"Don't stop!" they yelled.

And I didn't.

"Marry me!" proposed Tut. "These clams are Finest Kind!"

I smiled.

And kept baking.

This was, I decided, a blast!

And it hit me right then that there might be something for me in this food world. I had had a great day. People loved the food. Heck, I had been proposed to! It certainly bore exploring, especially if it meant I could stay on land. And, I realized, it could not possibly get much better than this. This was, to be sure, the very Finest Kind.

Chapter Twenty-Seven

Thanksgiving at Blueberry Hill

 Thanksgivings were never quite the same after we moved away from Vermont. My sisters and I tried. One year Heather came to visit me and Lucinda while we were still in Evanston. Lucinda was a senior at Northwestern University. I was a senior at Evanston Township High School and had been living with Lucinda in our little apartment on Main Street for a year by then. That might have been the year that we decided to go and have a spaghetti dinner. One year we went to a coffee shop and had hot turkey sandwiches. And then one year we decided that to even try to recreate this Blueberry Hill day was just too hard.

One year we did try. Lucinda and I cooked for three days. We made Apple, Pumpkin, and Pecan Pies, Cranberry Relish and Apple Chutney. We made Acorn Squash and Butternut Squash and a Zucchini Casserole, Sweet Potatoes, Mashed Potatoes, and even a Layered Potato Gratin. We made Cranberry Walnut Bread, Banana Bread, a Dilled Cheddar Bread, and Old-Fashioned Yeast Rolls. Finally, we made two different turkeys: one stuffed with Blueberry Hill Sausage and Sage Bread Stuffing, and one that my sister completely boned before filling with some exotic concoction she'd read about in *Gourmet* magazine. We made every bit of our traditional Blueberry Hill Thanksgiving meal and much more on top of that. We invited my sister's husband's family, a loud Italian gang from the south side of Chicago. We cooked and cooked and cooked, decorated our little apartment, and shined the place until it shimmered. Right at two o'clock on Thursday afternoon, much earlier than when my family was used to eating, but exactly when the in-laws demanded, my brother-in-law's family came in. His mother looked around, sniffed, and, I don't remember, but might have said that it smelled good. I do clearly remember that his father came in, looked around, sniffed, and snorted, "Where're the olives!"

"Olives?" my sister and I looked at each other. "Olives?"

The rest of the day was a disaster. We had no olives, nor did we, as it turned out, have *any* of the things Ed's family was used to. We had no packaged stuffing, no corn and bean casserole, and no bang-on-the-counter refrigerated biscuits. It was like we were a family from Mars.

Ed's family hated our food, picking and poking and, well, not eating. No olives! We were devastated. I don't even remember enjoying the enormous amount of leftovers we had amassed.

By the time I got to college, my sisters and I, busy, led our own lives. There were many years when we did not even see each other for this holiday. Heather was often involved in rehearsals for the improvisational theatre company she worked for in Boston. I also worked in the theatre, backstage, and sometimes our technical crews worked right straight through holidays like Thanksgiving. Someone might have made us turkey, but I don't remember. We probably went to the sandwich vendor and had tuna subs. Thanksgiving just was not very important to any of us right then.

But after college, when I moved to New York to continue my theatre studies, I cooked my first turkey. I lived near enough to Central Park West that Thanksgiving Eve turned into all-night watch-them-blow-up-the-balloons-for-the-Macy's-Thanksgiving-Day-parade extravaganzas. On the mornings of those Thanksgivings, my roommates and I would bundle up and shuffle over to watch the parade. A turkey, cooking away back in the apartment, was not the focus.

Always my favorite day as a child, I learned to wish for the whole thing to just pass. Each year, when the day drew near, I tried not to think about waking up in the bedroom above the kitchen at Blueberry Hill to the fragrant onions and celery sautéing on my mother's stove. My sisters and I didn't need prompting or an alarm clock once those aromas reached us. Up we'd hop, scrambling into our clothes and down to the kitchen to help make Thanksgiving Dinner at Blueberry Hill. There were certainly guests coming and we had a lot to do!

Bread, which had sat out on the counter all night, needed to be torn into small pieces for the stuffing. Chestnuts, hot from the oven, needed to be peeled. The turkey needed to be stuffed and sewn up and seasoned and covered and tucked into the oven. Pies needed to be made, cream whipped, tables set. Thanksgiving Day at Blueberry Hill was the most special day for us. A whole day of my sisters and I and our mother cooking together in the kitchen. My father hovered around, whistling and honing his carving knife.

But after my sisters and I had moved away, after we tried, and failed, to recreate the day and after we tried, and failed, to come up with an alternative celebration, and after we tried, and failed, to adapt to other families, we just finally stopped trying.

Until, that is, the year when I got to go back and cook at Blueberry Hill one last time.

Some time in October my half sister had called from Vermont. She had moved to the hunting camp she and her husband had built right on the edge of the Blueberry Hill property. She had, she said, decided to have all the Goshen stragglers over for a Thanksgiving Dinner. Tony, the owner of Blueberry Hill, had taken the day off and was going hiking with turkey sandwiches. The kitchen, my mother's kitchen, would be mine for the day.

"You want to come up and cook?" Diane said. "There'll be about twenty people. You can have the run of the kitchen. I'll set the table if you'll cook."

Would I! A surge of energy coursed through me. Cooking at Blueberry Hill. My dream. Cooking in my mother's kitchen. On my mother's stove. With, maybe, my mother's pots and pans.

I had been back to Blueberry Hill a couple of times since we'd moved away, but the Inn was always filled with Tony's guests and staff. I never had enough time, or enough privacy, to wander around as much as I wanted to. I would have liked to sit on a stool and run my hands over the counters, the tables, the walls, even. But, on those few occasions when I'd been back, there had never been enough time.

"You bet!" I yelped. "You don't need to ask me again!"

I could hardly wait for the day. I started making lists of groceries, recipes, memories. I sent the list to Diane so that, by the time I arrived from North Carolina, everything was there, waiting.

"Put me to work!" Diane chirped. "I brought an apron. A knife. Friends. Tell us what to do!" She waved her arms at the neighbors, all standing ready to be told what to do.

"Um," I stammered. "I don't really need any help."

"What're you talking about!," Diane protested, "Of *course* you need help!"

"No," I said, "I mean, no thanks, I really want to cook alone. But, um, how about if you set the tables, go collect flowers, chill the wine. If I need anything, I'll call you."

I couldn't wait for her to get out of the room. It had nothing to do with her. It had nothing to do with anyone. I just wanted to be in my mother's kitchen. Alone.

Diane gathered the friends and herded them into the dining room. For a few minutes I listened as they argued about the table placement and whether or not to make seating cards. About when they had decided to let everyone sit wherever they wanted, I drifted away. The voices faded. And there I was. Finally. Alone in my mother's kitchen.

I ignored the dried flowers that Tony's wife had hung upside down from the ceiling. And I did not pay attention to the newly redecorated porch which looked a whole lot like a photo shoot from *House Beautiful*. I closed out all the improvements and let myself drift. In my mind I could see my mother's books, no longer on the shelves, the recipes which were no longer painted on the walls, the little soft-boiled-egg-warmer dolls that used to sit in front of my mother's things. All of my mother's things had been replaced by Tony's books, paintings, and things.

But at that moment, it didn't matter.

I went to the counter. Unpacked the groceries and lined them up. Sausage, bread, onions, celery, wine, a turkey, sweet potatoes, cranberries, Brussels sprouts, grapes, pumpkin, mince-meat, flour, sugar, butter. I went to work.

I rummaged around and found bowls and knives and measuring tools. I tore up the bread, sautéed the onions, the celery, made stuffing, filled the bird, seasoned it, wrapped it, and put it in to bake. Put it in to bake in my mother's oven.

Finally I had all the time I wanted. I made Cranberry Sauce. Sweet Potatoes with Maple Syrup, Brussels Sprouts with Green Grapes and Browned Butter. I made a Pumpkin Pie. Elsie's Biscuits. I filled the kitchen with my own fragrances, with my mother's fragrances.

"Time to get up, girls," I could almost hear my mother's voice. "Lucinda! Heather! Laurey!!! Time to help make Thanksgiving Dinner!"

But this time it was me, all alone, hypnotized by it all. This time it was me browning the sausage and creating. I was the one in control of the stove. I was the one whose food would be served that night. My food. Made in my mother's oven.

The time evaporated. At some point Diane's friends came into the kitchen, asked if I needed help, and seeing that I didn't, left. And a few hours later, they all came back, all dressed up and ready for dinner. Their husbands and boyfriends, awkward in pressed shirts, shuffled into the dining room. The town stragglers filed in too, taking their seats at Diane's tables.

I had, by this time, finished cooking. Had moved everything into the dining room, and arranged it on platters on a buffet in front of the huge fireplace where, my father had once pointed out, a jewel lurked behind a piece of quartz. Later someone told me it was a geode, but I preferred the image of jewels. It seemed to twinkle as I set out the dinner.

"Wow!" Diane exclaimed. "You did all this alone?"

I didn't bother saying anything. She'd seen me in there by myself.

"Well, friends, let's eat!"

And they did.

Later, Tony and his wife came home from the hike. Tony surveyed the remnants of the dinner.

"Want to come cook here?" he asked. "Now that'd be something, wouldn't it? Elsie's daughter cooking at Blueberry Hill! What a coup!"

"Oh, *yes*!" I gushed. "Yes, I want to cook here! Yes. Please!!!"

"Really?" Tony said. And then, after a moment, "No. It'd never work. You'd be miserable. You need to do your own thing. I couldn't let you do it."

I pleaded and begged. Nothing had felt so good to me for such a long time. All I wanted, I had discovered, was to be back there in my mother's kitchen, cooking in the embrace of that oven. But Tony had stopped listening. He'd been joking, he said. Hadn't really meant it. No, I'd have to go back to North Carolina. My mother's kitchen was no longer available. You can't go home again. I desperately wanted to. But my mother's kitchen now belonged to Tony. And that was the end of that story.

Just like the little packets of jelly, I carried the turkey around with me for a few days, bringing it with me if I went visiting during that Thanksgiving vacation, making sandwiches and casseroles and then a rich soup with it. And finally, of course, we'd eaten all of it, and it was time to pack up and go back to my own home, my own books, and my own tiny, rented apartment's kitchen.

It was time, finally, to start out on my own.

Chapter Twenty-Eight

Cooking for 200

"Here you go," the kitchen manager at Esalen directed me and a clutch of "work-scholars" to a counter, "you can peel garlic." She handed us a crate of fat, white heads of garlic, gave us little finger bowls of hot water ("you can rinse your fingers in the water when they get sticky") and showed us how we could smash the cloves with a ketchup bottle, making it easy to peel the garlic. "And when you've finished, you can clean these cases of broccoli."

I was crazily giddy. Wow! Look at all the stainless steel! Look at the huge pots and pans. Look at the gigantic butcher block tables. Even the stacks of aprons seemed exotic. I pulled a pile of garlic bulbs to my side of one of the work tables and began to separate the cloves, putting papery husks in one pile for the compost bin and collecting the ready-to-be-smashed cloves in another towering pile. In a snap, mine were all ready for clobbering, which I did with gusto, popping each clove just exactly hard enough to make the outer paper crack. I did them one at a time but in a very orderly fashion: my very own mini assembly line. I had read about efficiency experts, and I could tell I had created one in myself. Separate all the cloves. Pound all the cloves. Peel all the cloves.

Done!

I glanced over at my fellow work-scholars. We were eight of some thirty-odd folks spending a month at Esalen Institute, perched on the edge of the ocean in Big Sur, California. We paid a smaller amount of tuition than the regular seminarians, in exchange for working at the Institute. We ran the garden, took care of the grounds, cleaned the rooms, and did all the customary kitchen tasks. At night our group met and experienced the mind, body, and spiritual offerings of the month: a crash course in alternative healing, thinking, living, and imagining. Most people there were searching for meaning in one way or another. We were each on a quest. The work was a part, but personal growth, I could see, was the goal.

I was searching too.

After a number of years of living in New York City, working backstage in the world of theatrical lighting, I was sick of that life. I was ready for a change. I was done with lighting, sick of the theatre, unhappy with my work and life in New York. Wondering what else I could do, I had taken an Outward Bound course and, as these things happen, had met someone who had told me about someone else who, when we met, told me about Esalen. I, not knowing what else to do, had listened and followed and ended up on a quest that, at the moment, had led me to Esalen as a work-scholar in the kitchen, peeling cloves of garlic. I was thrilled!

On day two, the cook greeted us, guided us through an "attunement session" where we all held hands and stood in a circle, grounding ourselves and "getting our spirits in the same place" before she directed us to our work tables and our crates of garlic and broccoli. Once again, I dove into the task, gleefully separating, smashing, and peeling my allotment. I was done way ahead of everyone else.

"You're *fast!*" one of my coworkers said. "Slow down! What's the hurry? Breathe. Be *with* the garlic. You're being so task oriented. Trust the process."

I scowled—to myself that is. After all, we were an attuned group, right? Scowling was not appropriate. No one else, it was true, was anywhere near as fast as I. And no one looked like they were interested in speeding up. I considered helping them, but did not want to interrupt their conversations about chakras and auras and such. It's not that I didn't want to talk about those things. I was learning a lot at night in our classes and seminars. But now, it seemed, was time to peel garlic.

On the third day, after our attunement circle, the cook pointed out the day's task to the group: more garlic and more broccoli. I wondered when everyone was going to get sick of peeling garlic and cleaning broccoli, though I didn't say anything. Just as I started to sit down to tackle my assignment, the cook winked at me and asked if I'd like to try something else.

I jumped up. Would I!

"What would you like to make?" she asked. "You look like you know what you're doing. How about making dinner tonight?"

"Dinner? For *everyone*?" I sputtered. "I mean, really? *Really*, truly? Um, how many people are there?"

"Two hundred or so," she said, nonchalantly.

"Two hundred!!!??? Wow! What shall I make?" Two hundred, how do you cook for 200? I'd cooked for myself. Some. And for a friend or two—maybe four at the most. I knew how to make brownies. And I was pretty good at fried eggs. But dinner for 200?

"How about if you make a Puttanesca"

"Sure, um, but, uh, what is a Puttanesca?"

"Here," she said, tossing me a fat cookbook, "it means 'whore' but really it's just a spicy marinara sauce. I think the recipe is for eight. Just multiply."

Multiply? Just *multiply*?! Wow! Cooking for 200 people! The last summer of Blueberry Hill, after we'd added on to the dining room, we could accommodate forty-five people and that, I recall, was a huge group to us. My mother would start cooking in the morning for such a group. But here it was the afternoon already, and I had just been invited to cook for 200! Boy oh boy! I didn't remember being this excited by anything in a long time.

My fellow work-scholars sat over at their table, slowly and painstakingly taking little shreds of paper off individual cloves of garlic. After each de-papering, they'd tap with a salt shaker—tap tap tap—all the while talking about vision quests and sweat lodges and gestalt therapy. And while that was interesting, I was glad to be away from the slowpokes and thrilled to be involved in my big and very important project.

I was making dinner for 200 people. Tonight!

The cook pointed out the knives, the pots, some dried herbs grown on the property. She helped me locate tomatoes and even gave a pile of onions to the garlic tappers to peel and slice. For me!

The kitchen had a huge burner where one gigantic pot sat. I found a fat wooden spoon, gallons of olive oil, quarts of tomatoes, pounds of onions, and a big tub of capers that, if I'd wanted to, I could have scooped up by the fistful. I had a bucket of fresh basil and a mixing bowl full of peeled garlic from the work-scholars' tables. Acting as if I knew just what I was doing, I started sautéing the aromatic vegetables. This was *so* much fun! As I cooked the kitchen filled with the aromas.

"Yum! That smells good!" strangers said, as they wandered into the kitchen.

They're talking about *my* cooking! About *my* onions!

I stirred, teased, tasted, seasoned, and poured love into my pot full of sauce. I was cooking for 200!

"Okay," the cook said, when she saw that my sauce was doing well, "take a break. Go get in the hot tubs or take a walk. You need some rest. I'll finish up here."

"But," I stammered, not wanting to leave. "I'm fine. I don't need a break. Really."

"Nope," she held up her hand. "Go. A rest will be good for you. I've got this under control. Thanks, by the way. This looks great. You're a natural."

Reluctantly, I left the kitchen. I didn't *want* to rest, I realized. I felt so invigorated! This was better than any massage, any walk, or any hot tub soak. I had just cooked for 200! I shuffled down the hill to the hot tubs in a daze, took off my clothes, rinsed off in the shower, and went outside and joined the eclectic group soaking and talking about garden divas and astral projections and energy healing.

I just cooked dinner for all of you, I thought to myself. Wow!

That night at dinner I could hardly sit still. I stood in line at the buffet and then served myself a beautiful salad of baby greens, harvested that afternoon in the garden. My friend Linda was the "sprout gal" that session, so I made sure to take some of each of her babies. There were little golden cherry tomatoes, crisp cucumber slices, sunflower seeds, raisins, peppers, onions, all kinds of things fresh from the Esalen garden. The bread, hot from the oven, melted the butter that I slathered on. And there, at the end of the table, bubbling away in a chafing dish of its own, was my sauce. I looked around the room. Yup! Everyone in the whole dining room was eating *my* Puttanesca Sauce. My face flushed, my pulse quickened. I stood still, watching. Did they like it? It seemed so. Each table was filled with seminarians conversing with animation. ". . . vision quest . . . chakra balancing . . . massage . . . healing . . . reiki . . . salt rub . . ." And, at each table, everyone was eating *my* sauce.

It all felt very familiar. It all felt very good. And while I really liked my growing awareness and the education about so many parts of the mind, body, and spirit, what I really liked, what I affirmed that night, was cooking. Just cooking. Pure, simple cooking.

Chapter Twenty-Nine

Outward Bound

 "Let me tell you about the Feuilleté of Wild Mushrooms at Aureole," I taunted, stirring a pot of macaroni and cheese over the camp stove. A crew of students, MBA candidates from Wake Forest, sat on the ground listening. "The puffed pastry was amazingly light. Each layer flaked and was separate from the next. And, when you bit into it, the outside, crisp, melted on your tongue. The wild mushrooms were fresh. Oysters, chanterelles, morels, all gathered from the woods and tossed in butter with a splash of white wine, a toss of parsley, a shave of truffle on top."

It had taken two years but, after taking my initial Outward Bound course at the North Carolina school as a thirty-year-old, and studying hard at various schools of outdoor education, I was finally an Outward Bound instructor! Delighted to get out of New York, I had moved to Asheville, a lovely art town in the mountains of the western part of the state. My life was changing. Not toward food, but toward helping people realize their own personal potential. It was, I thought, exactly what I wanted to do. But in my daydreams, I kept drifting off to the world of food.

As most of the students watched, the evening's designated cook tended the pot. A gloopy mess bubbled over the small camping stove. Experimentally, the cook added more milk powder, more cheese, more water, slightly tinged orange from the iodine used to purify it. The students, hungry, waited, but no one looked overly eager to eat this conglomeration.

"Or let me tell you about the time I had tapas at The Ballroom," I continued. "You go in and sit at the bar if you like. The bartender brings you a straight-sided little fist-size glass of sherry, dry. You sip and gaze at the platters full of Spanish hors d'oeuvres. It is an unbelievable display: roasted sweet peppers shiny from a drizzle of olive oil; tiny whole anchovies, barely grilled and glistening with freshly squeezed lemon; tiny slivers of potatoes—so thin you can see through them. Sausages and hams hang from the ceiling and, in case you don't see what you want—though I can't imagine how that would be—you can order things: shrimp with the heads still on, which come to you sizzling and sputtering in their garlic and butter bath; blood pudding—disgusting but, heck, you're having a food adventure so you can try everything, right?"

"Stop!" my students yelled, "This is torture!"

But I couldn't stop. I couldn't stop thinking about those meals I'd eaten for the past three years in New York when I was finally earning enough money to be able to afford to go out to dinner on a fairly regular basis. After some ten years in lighting, I had been working as a commercial interior designer in the toy industry, creating and building showrooms for major toy manufacturers. Remember My Little Pony? GI Joe? Charmkins? (Okay, unless you knew a little girl in 1985 you've probably never heard of these perfumed little dolls that were toys "and jewelry!") But how about Transformers, those Japanese imports that changed from a robot to an airplane? Well, I was one of the people who built the showrooms where toy buyers who came to New York to see them saw them. And at Toy Fair time, all the stops were pulled out. Money flew like confetti. And the team of us, the "visual merchandisers," got to go out to dinner with the bosses.

"Oh, the *kaiseki* we had at Nippon!" I continued. "Now that was a meal!"

That time the boss, the company president in fact, had taken us all to the top-rated Japanese restaurant in all of New York City and had waved to the waiter to bring us each a meal of "whatever the chef feels like making." From the brief glimpse I had at the menu, I think the price was $300—per person! In 1985! Exquisite plates arrived, one at a time, with tiny, perfect portions on them, each one a miniature Japanese still life: a fan of transparent slices of cucumber with a scattering of flying fish roe; three perfect slices of toro, the fatty meat from giant tuna; five thumbnail-size crabs—fried whole and served marching across each plate, a thimbleful of wasabi horseradish, sculpted to look like a pebble, sitting on the side.

"Here, who's ready for dinner?" I sat and watched the student ladling macaroni slop into their tin cups. Not seeing what we were about to eat, I smiled as I remembered those extravagant New York meals.

"Montrachet was wonderful too," I continued to the students now eating the gloopy pasta. "We had the lobster with a lemon cream. It was so good I could have licked the plate. And then there was Arcadia," my voice trailed off.

The students finished their macaroni and scrubbed their cups with pine needles, swirling iodine water to rinse, mindful that the water had been collected, drop by drop, earlier in the day, funneled into the water bottles using rhododendron leaves.

The next day was the day for the ropes course. My mind was mostly with the students, but drifted off when no one was near my perch high in the trees. I had to sit and wait while they maneuvered through the aerial obstacle course until they made their way to me at the "butt box." When they reached me, after walking across the balance beam, through the cargo net, and under the crisscross "spider's web," I had to hook their harnesses up to the zip line, checking and double checking the double carabiners to make sure they were well tied in. We didn't want to drop anyone from the fifty-foot-high platform. By the time they reached me, at the end of the difficult course, they were either very confident or shakingly terrified.

"You can do this," I soothed a particularly terrified one. "Think of how good you'll feel when you make this move, when you take the step off this platform. You have seen others students go. You have watched me check your safety system. You *know* you can do this. Okay, tell me. If you knew you could do *this*, what *else* could you imagine doing?"

The student shook, burst into tears, and splurted out a story about a boss or a boyfriend or an unmet challenge, sobbing that if she could summon the courage to jump here, that might mean she could deal with her boss later.

"I don't want to do this anymore," I thought to myself, trying to concentrate on the quaking student. "I want to explore that food. I want to make Feuilleté of Wild Mushrooms." I shook my head vigorously. I had to pay attention! The student was crying and needed me! Daydreaming about food would have to wait. Focus on the student. Be in *this* moment! Coax. Cajole. Convince.

An excruciating amount of time passed and finally the student slid off the platform, swinging in a huge arc at the end of the line, screaming at the top of her lungs. I felt relief, not that she had jumped, but from knowing I could return to my thoughts of those meals.

"I can't do this anymore," I said to myself after a summer full of courses. "I need to be doing something with food. I don't want to facilitate one more person's peak experience. I need to change my own life."

Full of Outward Bound bravado, "if I can climb rocks blindfolded I can *certainly* open a restaurant," I announced to my sisters that I was done with Outward Bound instructing and was on to the world of food.

"I'm going to open a restaurant!" I announced to my sisters. "Blueberry Hill South."

"Don't you remember how hard Mommy and Daddy worked?" shrieked Lucinda. "Don't be ridiculous. A restaurant? You are crazy! If you insist on doing anything in the food world, I think you should just start by catering."

"Right," I replied, discouraged at her lack of enthusiasm for my new idea. "How do you do catering?"

I'd never been to a catered party, never been to a catered wedding—all of my friends were single and working either in the theatre in New York or as itinerant Outward Bound instructors.

"Join the Junior League," Lucinda suggested. "Give them a party. You can cook. You'll be fine. Just start. But I really think the restaurant is a bad idea."

I had hardly heard of Junior League and, once I looked into it, I realized that Women Mean Business, a local networking group, was a better organization for me to join. For one thing, I didn't own any nice clothes except for my Outward Bound outdoor gear, very casual and not nearly spiffy enough for that fancy group of women. Women Mean Business was much less formal and I felt it was a good place to start.

"We have a meeting in two weeks," the membership director told me. "There'll be time at the end of the meeting for newcomers to stand up and introduce themselves. Come join in!"

I spent the next two weeks making a flyer. "Having a party?" I wrote, "Give me a call!"

When the time came for the meeting I was sweating with fear. I had twenty brochures. I had a clean shirt. Clean pants. Clean shoes. My Outward Bound clothes were put away for the time being. And at the end of the meeting, when it came time for introductions, I stood up, summoned my best "you can do this" pose and introduced myself.

"My name is Laurey Masterton," I said. "I am new in Asheville and I have a new catering business. I'd love to help you if you ever need to have anything catered. Just give me a call."

The members smiled politely, but no one called.

I went back and instructed another Outward Bound course trying to be content, but it did not take long for the daydreaming to start again.

"Arcadia, now *that* was a meal! Sitting at those white clothed tables, gazing at Paul Davis's wraparound mural, swooning over the risotto. Amazing." This story was offered over a bag of toasted Corn Nuts. Or it could have been accompanied by stale bagels and hard peanut butter. Perhaps it was served with burned chili, courtesy of an inept and inattentive student. "I'll always count that as one of the best meals of my life."

At the end of the course I went back to Asheville. How am I going to do this?, I thought.

My sister's advice came back to me. Give them a party!

Which is exactly what I did. I made little puffs of smoked salmon-filled bites, cherry tomatoes with Gorgonzola filling, tiny cookies, salty snacks, and sweets too. I went to Pier One, bought a bunch of cheap baskets, sprayed them black, and did my best to make an interesting presentation. To my delight, the members were impressed. One person called me. Could I do a lunch for fifty? Sure I could!

I was off and running. I was going to be a caterer!

Chapter Thirty

Congo Bars

 It *really* started with Congo Bars, the I-am-going-to-cook-for-a-living, that is.

"You cook?" said my new friend, my new North Carolina landlady, Elizabeth Ann, almost as soon as she met me. "You want to cook me a birthday dinner? My birthday's in a few days! And I love to eat, but I don't cook."

"Would I!" I jumped at her proposal. "Sure thing, I'll cook for you! What do you like?"

"Surprise me," she said, "I like everything! And I am going to invite some friends. Say, eight or nine people, okay?"

"You bet!" I chirped. Yay! Cooking!

Now, *this* was fun. I consulted my collection of cookbooks—all five of them—and after I'd come up with a festive menu, I scurried down the steps of my apartment, hopped into my bright orange VW van, scooted over to the fancy grocery store and loaded up with fresh trout, beautiful produce, and ingredients for a cake. I piled everything into the van, drove home, skipped up the stairs to my apartment with bags of food and plunged in. I created a rice and dried fruit filling for the trout, made a delicious layered vegetable gratin with the fresh produce, and whipped up my mother's Perfect White Cake for dessert. And, in honor of the day in early July, I topped the cake with blueberries, whipped cream, and strawberries.

The time flew by.

I was very very happy.

The guests arrived.

Ate.

Exclaimed.

"Where did you come from?"

"Where did you learn how to cook?"

"This is delicious!"

"This is the best meal I've ever had in my life!"

I floated on the compliments. These words were the same ones that guests at Blueberry Hill had said to my mother and now they were saying them to me!

"I learned by watching my mother," I said, telling them a little bit about the Inn. "This is the way I grew up."

"Wow!" said one of the women, one whom I had never met before that night, "you are *good*! I think you should open up a restaurant! Come see me tomorrow and I'll give you a book to read. It'll tell you how to do it, open a restaurant, that is. My name is Pickett, by the way. Come see me at my café tomorrow. It's underneath Malaprops, the bookstore. Right downtown."

"Really?" I squeaked. "Do you mean it?"

She did, she said, and so I found myself in her office in the back of her small café the next morning. I sat on a milk crate, watching as she shuffled produce orders and candy samples. I stared at shelves filled with fat bags of coffee beans and jars of mayonnaise and boxes of napkins.

This, I said to myself, is where I want to be. Surrounded by this stuff.

"Here," my new friend said, "read this book."

She gave me Margaret Fox's *Café Beaujolais*, a cookbook with lots of details on how she had gotten started in her small yet very successful restaurant. I had never heard of her before that moment, but at a glance, I was captivated. I flipped through the pages, thanked Pickett, tucked the book under my arm, scampered through the café, out the door, across the deck, down the stairs, and into my van, and hurried home where I inhaled the words. She'd begun, she related, by making Congo Bars—blonde brownies—which she'd sold to the art movie theatre in her town.

This is it! I thought. Here's my answer. My start. If it worked for Fox, I reasoned, it'll certainly work for me! We didn't have an art movie theatre, but we had Malaprops Café! Surely *they'd* buy my Congo Bars. I could see it all spread out before me, a sweet path to my certain success. And, most important, it was my way out of Outward Bound. I had only one more course scheduled. I'd better figure out something soon.

Once again I made a grocery list, skipped down the stairs, hopped in my VW van, hustled over to the fancy grocery store, bought all the ingredients for Congo Bars, went to Complements to the Chef, Asheville's amazing fancy cooking implement store, bought a double insulated baking pan, and zipped home.

I followed the recipe exactly, mixing the ingredients in the spanking new red Kitchen Aid mixer my sisters had given me the previous Christmas. The last time I had baked was in seventh grade—those brownies, you remember—so I was careful to measure, mix, spread, and bake the way the book instructed. I was not used to following recipes, preferring to ad lib. But these, I predicted, were going to change my life, so I'd better do them exactly the way they were written. I popped them into the oven.

Boy, they smelled good! I paced, glancing through the oven door like a worried mother. They rose and turned a beautiful golden brown. Yes, I told myself, these are magic!

I could barely wait until they were cool before I cut into a corner of the pan. Ah! This was, indeed, my ticket, I thought. These were incredible! The best ever. My path to fame and fortune. Just like Margaret Fox. I was on my way!

"Elizabeth Ann! Elizabeth Ann!" I yelled down the steps to my landlady's apartment. "I've got it! I've figured it all out. Listen to this," I related the story of Pickett and the book and the recipe and my idea for selling the Congo Bars. I told her about how it was my way out of Outward Bound and the way to my lifelong dream. I gushed, "I'm going to sell Congo Bars at Malaprops Café downtown. Margaret Fox did it in Mendocino and now look at her! She has a cookbook, a restaurant. She's famous and it all started with Congo Bars!"

Elizabeth Ann smiled at me. "Laurey Loo," she said, "you are something else. Good luck!"

I forced myself to wait for the bars to cool all the way down before I finished cutting and wrapping them. My orange VW van waited outside. I piled my wrapped Congo Bar squares into a bag, skipped down my stairs, hopped into the car, and sped to my new friend's café.

"Here!" I burst out as I exploded into her office, interrupting a meeting.

Pickett looked up, frowning.

"Yes?" she sniffed. "I'm in a meeting."

"Yes, I see, but you *have* to try these! Congo Bars. Right from the book. You know, *Café Beaujolais*. I was, um, thinking you might like to sell them in the café."

Pickett looked at the salesman, shrugged at him with an apologetic look, turned to me, took one of the bars, unwrapped it, looked at it, pinched it, sniffed it, and then bit into it. I waited expectantly, giddy.

"This is awful!" she blurted. "It's raw!"

I froze. I could not speak.

"Um."

"I mean, yuck!" she continued, scowling, "It tastes like paste."

"But I followed the recipe exactly," I stammered.

I did not know what else to say.

"Well," she said dismissively, "I don't like them."

She turned back to the salesman.

I picked up the bag with my future in it, turned, and left the room. As I walked through the café I made sure not to look at anyone. I was positive they all knew I had been rejected. I was certain they could see what a failure I was, all of a sudden.

I slipped out the back door, crossed the deck, padded down the steps, opened my van door, got in, and drove slowly home. I parked my van next to Elizabeth Ann's truck, and tried to slink upstairs.

But Elizabeth Ann heard me.

"How'd it go?" she asked, excited for me.

Instead of answering I burst out crying.

"She *hated* them" I blurted, collapsing onto her stairs. "Hated them! And I interrupted her in a meeting and she was mean to me and I'll *never* get anywhere and I can't even cook and so what am I going to do in my life? What am I going to do?" I was sobbing by then.

"Oh Laurey Loo," she soothed. "Just because *one* person doesn't like *one* thing, well, you can't just listen to that one person. Do *you* like the Congo Bars?"

"Yes," I sniffed, trying to calm down, "I do, I really do."

"Well then, you need to listen to yourself. You'll figure it out. You really will. Now give me one of those things and let's go for a hike!"

And so we did.

(Oh, by the way, when I opened my own shop, I made and sold these very Congo Bars—with excellent results. I still undercook them. It's just the way I like 'em!)

Congo Bars
The Recipe

And so here it is: the Congo Bar recipe. I make sure they stay on the menu here at Laurey's. We send them out on lots of parties and keep the cookie station filled with them. They continue to be my favorites. And I still make sure they're slightly undercooked. Yum. Here again I suggest you weigh the ingredients.

Makes 24 bars

The ingredients:

14 ounces butter (3 ³/₄ sticks)
6 large eggs
2 pounds light brown sugar
1 teaspoon table salt
1 pound plus 10 ounces all-purpose flour

1 tablespoon baking powder
2 ²/₃ cups chocolate chips
2 cups chopped walnuts

Here's what you do: Preheat the oven to 325°F. Grease and flour a baking sheet (18 x 13 x 1-inch).
Melt the butter and set it aside to cool.

Using an electric stand mixer with the paddle attachment, combine the eggs, sugar, and salt, mixing using a low speed until the blend is no longer granular—a couple of minutes. Add the cooled butter to the egg mixture, keeping the mixer running. Sift the flour and baking powder together and add to the butter-sugar-egg mixture. Add the chocolate chips and nuts and mix on high for 45 seconds. Spread in the prepared baking pan..

Bake at 325°F until the center tests done. A toothpick inserted in the center of the pan can still be slightly moist. In our oven this takes 35 minutes but as I said before, do keep your eye on them the first time, because all ovens are really very different. In my opinion, it is essential not to cook them until they are fully baked. I usually stop them when the edges are almost done. I like them on the underdone side.

Cool on a cooling rack. Cut into 24 bars. Enjoy!

Note: This recipe will make 2 dozen full-size Congo Bars, though you can easily cut them smaller. But you already knew that.

Thanks to Margaret Fox for permission to use her recipe for Congo Bars, printed originally in <u>Café Beaujolais</u>, printed in 1984 by Ten Speed Press.

Chapter Thirty-One

Apple Tart Upset

 "What's the worst thing that ever happened to you as a caterer?" Ah, the favorite question. As you might imagine, after all these years in this profession, I have a collection of stories. Nothing really *horrible* has ever happened to me (though I have a colleague in California who actually did have the guest of honor die during a party—ugh!) but there have been a number of funny (um, mostly funny) things that I can relate. Here's one.

It was in my early days as a caterer. I was catering a party for twenty-four people in a client's home. I had a brand new assistant, so new that I had never even met her before I got to the party. The dessert was an Apple Tart with Sour Cream Sauce. Dinner went along just fine with my new helper doing a good enough job, keeping up with the guests' needs and being an adequate helper.

During the dinner, I put the three Apple Tarts into the oven to warm. When it came time for dessert, I took one out and prepared to cut it. Tart pans, as you know, have a flat bottom disk that is a separate piece from the fluted edge piece. Since it is easier to cut the tart without the fluted edge piece, one generally removes it before cutting the tart.

I took the first tart from the oven and laid it on the counter top. I slid the whole tart to the edge of the counter, put my hand under the disk part and picked it up, letting the fluted edge part drop down a bit, which made it possible to take the fluted edge and set it aside. I then put the disk part, with the tart still on it, back on the counter, where I cut and served eight pieces of tart, first adding a dollop of the vanilla sour cream sauce and giving the plates to my helper to serve.

"Gosh, that was time consuming!" I noted to myself. I turned to take the second tart out of the oven.

Feeling very smart and efficient, I decided to save the pesky step of sliding the tart to the edge of the counter to remove the fluted edge part.

"I'll just take the fluted edge part off in the oven!" I chortled to myself. This way I could just carry the tart on its disk over to the counter and cut it and serve it from there. "I'll save a step!"

I opened the oven door and inched the tart to the front of the oven rack. I put my right hand under the disk and let the fluted edge part drop off.

"Yeeeooowwwww!!!" I yelped. The fluted edge part, right out of the oven, was *very hot* and it had slipped all the way down onto my arm and was—yipes!—*burning* me! My right hand contracted. My fingers sprung open. The tart flew up into the air, did a lovely end-over-end turn, and landed face down on the oven door with a stomach-turning SPLAT!

My new helper took one look and headed for the kitchen door. "I'll go out to clean the ashtrays," she said. (See how long ago this was?)

I stared at my upside-down tart. I had twenty-four guests. I had brought three tarts. Each tart had eight pieces. I had just twenty-four pieces for the twenty-four guests. I was in trouble.

When my helper returned from ashtray patrol, the tart was still planted, face down, on the oven door. There was nothing to do but to pick the thing up, turn it over, and reconstruct it as well as possible. We did our best, our four hands working four pancake turners into an awkward rescue operation. The sour cream sauce helped hide our patches.

For the third tart I went back to my first method, taking the pan to the counter, letting it sit, scooting it to the edge of the counter, and so on. This time I was especially careful not to burn myself as I separated the disk part from the fluted edge part. It took more time, but the service proceeded uneventfully.

In the end, none of the guests suspected anything had happened, but more important, this is where my motto "Always Bring Extra Sauce" started. Ah, catering!

Chapter Thirty-Two

The Perfect White Cake

The second in the series of stories I tell when people ask about catering disasters is this one. It is, as are the others, completely true though the names have been changed (you'll see why). I got through it and moved on, but it did take some time before I felt comfortable listening to the phone messages after a weekend away from work.

It shouldn't have been that big of a deal. All they wanted was a wedding cake. Simple.

Diane and her future stepdaughter Constance, an angry-looking teenager, showed up one afternoon. They had called ahead of time and had made an appointment to talk to me about Diane and Constance's father's wedding. Diane, thinking no doubt that it would be a good step-motherly thing to do, had invited Constance to help plan this one small part of the wedding that was going to be held in a few weeks.

"What kinds of cake do you recommend?" Diane asked me, looking at Constance.

"Oh, pretty much whatever you like," I answered. "Chocolate, Orange Almond, Lemon Poppy Seed, Italian Nut. All the standards. Or perhaps you might like our Perfect White Cake. It is really a very nice cake. My mother made it for all of our birthdays when my sisters and I were growing up. I love it. We would decorate it with a butter and confectioner's sugar frosting."

"What do you think, honey?" Diane asked Constance, who sat sullenly in her chair.

Constance shrugged.

"Orange Almond?" Diane asked.

Shrug.

"Your Dad likes Chocolate. Mmmm, maybe let's do Chocolate. What do you say?"

Shrug.

"Or, well, maybe we should just stick with White after all, do you think?" Diane was really trying. "Most people like white cake. How 'bout white, Sweetie?"

Constance winced.

"Okay. White Cake it is. Great!" Diane caught my eye. Shook her head slightly.
Constance looked at the floor.

"How many people will there be?" I asked Constance.

Constance shrugged her shoulders.

"About fifty, I think, don't you, Constance?"

Shrug.

I could feel my neck tensing.

"And this wedding is going to be . . .?" I prompted Constance.

"At the Club," Diane blurted.

"Right! And the wedding starts at . . .?" again I questioned Constance. I wanted this meeting to be over.

Constance stared out the window of my shop.

"At six, but we'll be eating dinner before the cake, of course, right, Constance?" Diane said.

Constance—no surprise—said nothing.

"The Club," I said. "Fine." I pictured the Club, a big old building near the golf course. The Club, Diane said, would be making all the food, but they wanted us to do the cake.

Diane and I talked about what the cake would look like, "with diagonal piping, some flowers, nothing too elaborate, just something simple," while Constance fidgeted, her knee bouncing, her fingers picking at her already raw-looking cuticles.

"Okay. We'll be there. Um, and congratulations." I said.

When the time came for the wedding weekend I became the baker. This was in the very early days of my business. I still baked, delivered, cooked, served. Everything. A cake for fifty people is not that big, but it took me a day to bake and a good part of another day to decorate. When I was done I was very pleased with my work. The cake looked just the way I had pictured it. Diane, at least, would be pleased. I took a photograph for my scrap book.

I did have a regular coworker named Monroe by then, who helped me do many things, including helping to deliver and set up things. When I finished it, he loaded the cake into the van, and drove away to deliver it. In an hour or so he returned.

"How'd it go?" I asked. "How did it look? Did you get it to the Club safely? Did it look good in the space? Did you see anyone?"

"It was fine," he said. "Some people were setting up the party and pointed me to the table. I set it up and left. It looked fine. Have a nice weekend. See you on Monday."

I left shortly after he did. I was excited because I was going camping for the weekend. I had my tent and pack all ready. No need to go home before I left with a friend to travel off to the mountains. I was excited about the break. I didn't get many breaks in those early years.

The weekend was, indeed, fun. No phones (this was before cell phones), no work, no worries. This was a break I had needed and it was good to be in the woods.

On Sunday, though, on my way home from camping, I decided to stop at the office to pick up a cookbook I had wanted to read. As I got to my desk, I saw my answering machine's light flashing. Hmm, four messages waited. Technically I was still off for the weekend, but curiosity prevailed and I pushed the "play messages" button.

I listened to the first one: "Hello, is this Laurey's Catering? This is the manager of the Country Club of Asheville. We're doing the Marshall wedding here this evening and we're just waiting for your cake. Give me a call when you get this message."

It seemed odd that I had not gotten that call before I left to go camping, but I assumed that Monroe must have shown up right after the manager called me.

But then I listened to the second message: "Hello, Laurey? Is anyone there? Can you pick up please? This is the Country Club of Asheville. The guests are arriving for the Marshall party. We're wondering when you are going to come with the cake. It is now five thirty."

My stomach turned over as I stood listening. Five thirty? Monroe had come back at three from his delivery. I played the message over. Oh. My. God. I realized in a flash that I had told him to go to the Grove Park Inn Country Club. The Marshall wedding was at the Country Club of Asheville. This was bad.

I kept listening: "Well, the ceremony has started. You're not here. The cake is not here. We can't just create a cake. We are planning to serve some leftover cupcakes we had from this morning's golf tournament. Please call when you get this message."

And finally: "They had cupcakes. You might want to call the Marshalls. Joseph is pretty upset. Have a nice weekend."

All the relaxation I had been feeling from *my* weekend evaporated in an instant. No cake? Cupcakes? What, I quaked, was going to happen now? What had they done? What was I going to do? Well, for one thing, I told myself, you're not going to do anything now. It was Sunday afternoon and that was that. I would have to wait until Monday at the earliest.

On Monday, when Monroe came in, I blurted out the disaster.

"What did they say when you delivered the cake?" I asked.

"They just told me to put it on the table. It did seem kind of small for that big table. It looked like they were having a huge wedding. But I just put it there and came back here."

When I called Joseph's office, I found out that Diane and Joseph were off for two weeks on a honeymoon. They were completely out of touch, not that I wanted to call them on their honeymoon—or ever, for that matter.

I called the Country Club of Asheville. Found out the minute by minute details. Listened as the manager told me how mad Joseph had been. How embarrassing it was for them all. How I was going to hear it when they got back.

And then I called the Grove Park Inn.

"How could you let the wrong cake get set up?" I demanded.

"How did we know?" the fellow I reached stammered. "I mean, when a *second* cake showed up we tried to call, but we didn't know where that first cake came from. So there was nothing we could do."

"Well," I sputtered, "what did you do with my cake?"

"We ate it. Liked it too!" he chirped. "We have your tray here. Come get it any time you want."

What could I say?

When Joseph and Diane finally got home, they had messages from me waiting at work and home. And, like a delinquent teenager, I was called to their house and had to sit and listen to a severe tongue-lashing. There was nothing I could say to make a difference. Of course I told them that their cake went to the wrong place. And of course I did not charge them. And, finally, I offered to make them another one. Which, thank heavens, they thought was a great idea!

So, a few weeks later, they invited all their guests back—just to eat cake. Everyone had fun. Got to hear all about the honeymoon. Got to laugh at the mix-up. And started a tradition that they continue: celebrating their real anniversary and then, a few weeks later, having a piece of cake. A piece of The Perfect White Cake.

Chapter Thirty-Three

Tiramisu

 Why is it that we are attracted to disasters? I suppose they are just more interesting than stories of how smoothly everything went. Here's the third one for you.

A new client named Jim, an older gentleman, came to my shop one day, and asked me to save a certain Monday, two months in the future, for a surprise party he wanted to give his wife in celebration of their twenty-fifth wedding anniversary. They had lived in Trieste, Italy for many years and he brought a complete menu of requests with him—all specific foods they had eaten during those years. He even had recipes which he told me he'd send, and he told me exactly how he wanted the meal served. He asked for three very specific and very authentic starters: a Minestrone Soup "they cook it for at least twelve hours!" he said, a *Pinzimonio* (basically a crudité assortment with olive oil for dipping), and a *Pomodoro*-something-or-other. Then he wanted a pasta course consisting of three different homemade pastas and three different sauces: a "cooked-for-hours" Marinara, a Pesto, and an Alfredo. For the main course, he requested whole trout filled with a raisin and stale Italian bread stuffing, a specialty of the region. "The bread *has* to be stale," he had emphasized. There was a salad course, a cheese course. The menu had many parts that were new to me at the time and I did not have any of the ingredients in my shop pantry, though I knew I could do it with this much time. I considered his suggestions, intrigued and excited about the challenge. He'd send the recipes later, he'd said.

"Oh! The dessert," he concluded triumphantly, "will be Tiramisu. Light as a feather! Just like the chef in Trieste made. Took him three days to make, as I recall. Anything less and the flavors won't meld correctly."

There was to be wine, rental tables and dishes and linens. We needed a full staff. And all of the special ingredients needed to be ordered. What fun!

"The guests will arrive on Monday at six thirty," he said. "And it is a surprise for Helen, so please don't call." I assured him we wouldn't, put all the papers in my notebook—my bible—and set my notebook on my desk. I made a note to order the food a few days ahead of time.

He called a month before the party, inquiring about the recipes. "Did you receive them?" "Yes," I replied. "They were now safely tucked in my notebook—my bible," I told him, knowing they were filed away because I would not need them until the week before the party when I would order the ingredients. I'd need the papers again on the day before the party when I would do the cooking. I meant to ask him about one special starter, that "Pomodoro" appetizer. Tomato something or other, I assumed. But he was in a hurry to get off the phone so I told myself I'd ask him the details later.

"And," he added just before hanging up, "would it be possible to move the party to Tuesday the twelfth?"

"Certainly," I replied. "Six thirty on Tuesday the twelfth it is. I'll take care of it." I took the papers out of my notebook, crossed out "Monday the 11th," wrote "Tuesday the 12th" on the top of the order sheet, and put the papers back in the book. I moved the ordering memo too. No need to get all this stuff too far in advance.

"Fine," he said.

"Yup," I agreed. "Anything else?"

"No, that's it."

Two weeks later, now two weeks before the party, Jim called again. I was in the midst of balancing my checkbook, paying bills, answering the phone, straightening my desk.

"Could you possibly move the party back to Monday night again?" he asked. "Some important friends can't make it on Tuesday. We'll need to switch back to Monday."

"Certainly," I replied, distracted and in the middle of my office's daily needs. "I'll change it in my book." I took the papers out of my book, put them on my desk, and continued with my day.

It was, as I remember, a very busy day, and I went to the kitchen to check in with the cooks, Peter and Kurt. I met with a couple of other clients, went to the bank, left in the middle of the day for a bit of exercise, came back, collected items for a party, served the party, and went home. I never straightened my desk, but after all, the party was not until next week, next—Tuesday, right? I reminded myself to check on that when I got back to work.

Later in the week I cleaned up my desk, reviewed the recipes, ordered the foods, planned for the rentals, the service, the surprise. Everything would be delivered first thing on Tuesday. Everything was set, I noted as I looked at my papers, for Tuesday. Tuesday it was, all tucked safely into my book—my bible.

And then, the next Monday, I confirmed everything with myself. I would get everything started first thing tomorrow morning. I had plenty of time. All was set for the next day. But then the phone rang. It was Jim.

"What time do you expect to arrive tonight?" he asked.

Tonight?

My stomach turned.

Tonight?

I was ready for the party—tomorrow!

"Just a sec, Jim," I spluttered, "let me change phones and go to my book."

Tonight?

I flew into my office, opened my book. I saw Monday scratched out, saw Tuesday replacing it and then remembered—I had never scratched out Tuesday and put Monday back in. I had put the party back in my book all right, but on Tuesday. Not Monday. It was Monday. It was the day of the party. Now what?

I ran out to the kitchen. "We have a situation here!" I blurted.

I ran back to my office. Picked up the phone. "Five thirty, Jim," I managed to squeak. "We'll see you in, um, a couple of hours."

Holy mazoly!!!

I ran back out to the kitchen. "Yup," I gasped, "a situation. I am going to go study this thing for a couple of minutes and then we're all going to have to go into full blast mode."

I went into my office, knees clanging together. I flipped through Jim's recipes. Fresh Trout. Three kinds of fresh pasta. Fresh Mozzarella. Mascarpone. Ladyfingers. Espresso. And three special sauces! And that *Pomodoro* thing, whatever the hell that was. I certainly could not call him back *now* to ask about it!

Monroe spun into high gear, jumping on the phones, arranging for the rental items and scrounging—and finding!—staff who were available for that night. Peter and Kurt, troopers both, went into a blur of cooking. I scooted to the store and bought the special items: the trout, the mascarpone, the ladyfingers, and, for good measure, some beautiful Roma tomatoes. But really, I thought, what a mess!

When I got back from shopping I threw the ingredients for the Tiramisu into a dish and tossed the whole thing into the refrigerator. Two days? Not a chance this time.

Amazingly, by five thirty the fellows had all the parts of the main meal assembled.

Miraculously, we were ready to at least get the first course served. We'd worry about the next course just before it was time. And maybe, I hoped, I'd be able to corner Jim and apologize for not being able to do the *Pomodoro* thing. I tossed all the dinner parts into boxes, threw them into the van, loading up anything else I could find that was vaguely Italian looking, including a bag of fresh basil, an extra loaf of bread, some extra mozzarella, and some olive oil. I collected the staff and took off to the party, explaining the situation as I drove.

We arrived at the same time as the rental and the staff flew to work, setting tables, organizing the service items, chilling the wine. Jim greeted us, smiled, and went home to collect his bride. He'd be back, he said, in a half hour.

"Okay," I peeped, "we'll be all set for you. I'm pleased that we were able to do everything, except, um, that *Pomodoro* thing. I'm so sorry, but I couldn't figure out what that was and there just never, um, was a good time to call you and ask about it."

He stopped still, turned around, and looked at me with wide, sad eyes—crestfallen, I could see, that this one piece would be missing. And then, by chance, his glance strayed to the box of ingredients on the counter, the box piled with the extraneous Italian items.

"But you have everything you need right there!" he said. "Bread, tomatoes, garlic, basil, and mozzarella! Put a piece of the cheese on a tomato, broil it, and put a basil leaf on top. That's all you need! *Bruschetta con Pomodoro!*"

He left to get himself ready. For me, things were beginning to look pretty good.

In the end, Helen was delighted and very happy. I managed to keep one course ahead of the guests, and the staff poured generous amounts of wine. Yes, she had been surprised, and, she reported, it was "exactly like what they'd eaten in those favorite spots in Trieste." Jim agreed. The starters, the soup, the pastas were all enjoyed. The salad was delicious, and the trout, they said, sublime. The Pomodoro was a delight. Jim ran around, encouraging everyone to have some. "Just like in Trieste!" he chortled.

Finally, even the Tiramisu made it to the table, perfectly set up as if it had been made days before. It was, the guests all said, perfect. Jim and Helen sparkled and cooed at each other. Twenty-five years celebrated exactly the way they wished.

At the end of it all I limped home. This, I said to myself, will be one for the book.
And so it is.

Chapter Thirty-Four

Buffets

 I have, at times, considered doing something else for work. I've imagined being a glassblower, but always decide that I really don't want to make my living as a studio artist (though I would like to putter at it someday). I day-dream about traveling and traveling and traveling until I can't stand it any-more and then writing about all the interesting people I've met, but then I wonder if I'd get bored or lonely, and how would I get enough money to do that, anyway? I contemplate returning to school to get a graduate degree but I can't figure out what to study and I am pretty comfortable in my house here and so, why would I go uproot myself like that?

In the end, I return to doing exactly what I am doing and realize I've been in training for this work almost my whole life. Often something will jolt me into this realization and I sigh and settle in and think, "Well, you can tweak what you are doing already, or you can adjust it, or you can flat out change it, but face it, it makes sense for you to have chosen to spend your life messing around with food. Might as well have fun with it!"

The other night I served a small dinner party in a lovely home near here. The guest of honor was the man of the house and the celebration was for his fifty-ninth birthday. It was a surprise party for him. Well, he knew he was going to have a party but he didn't know who was coming and he didn't know what we had decided to cook. As it turned out, all of the guests were fishing buddies of his so when I was discussing the menu with his wife we decided to make it a fish celebration. (Actually, I guess it could be considered a celebration for everyone but the fish!)

We started the dinner with two passed hors d'oeuvres: a Broiled Scallop on Crostini and then my mother's Shrimp Tempura with my father's Dunk Sauce. True to form, the shrimp were a wild hit, with people eating every single one I brought. They politely ate two of the scallop things (which were *very* good, if I do say so myself) but they didn't hesitate when we brought around the fourth round of the shrimp. I said a quiet thanks to my mother and father, and thought about the thousands of Shrimp Tempura my mother had made. "Still a big hit!" I whispered, smiling.

We served my mother's Barbecued Swordfish for the main course, a specialty at Blueberry Hill. I, for some reason, had never suggested it on a party. In the afternoon I went up to the kitchen at work and stirred the sauce. Yup! In a flash I was eight years old, standing at the grill at home, hoping that some sauce would be left for me after all the guests were served. There usually was. I loved that sauce, a simple barbecue sauce with ketchup and Worcestershire sauce and garlic (of course!) In my kitchen I stirred again, drizzled a couple of drops of sauce on my palm, tasted it, and nodded. Yes, that was the taste, still the same. Where else, I thought, could I have such instantaneous travel to another time of my life just by licking up a drip of a sauce.

For dessert, we served Mama's Sponge Cake with Sour Cream and Hot Blueberries. This, too, I had neglected to put on any menus recently, but it, too, was devoured. As John brought the plates into the kitchen, they were clean, a sure sign of a big hit. I thought of my grand-mother, "Mama," and wondered if she would ever have imagined that this cake of hers, that she learned from her mother in Russian would become a favorite for her daughter who cooked for people in Vermont and would be served, with deep love, by a granddaughter who owned a catering company in North Carolina?

As John served coffee, I washed the dishes. Normally I leave before dish time but this was a small party for important people and I was not in a big hurry, so I went back into my daydreaming as I soaped and rinsed each of the client's beautiful glasses and pieces of antique silverware. Without even thinking about what I was doing, as I dried each piece I made an arrangement of knives and spoons and glasses. I found myself putting the forks in a perfect row, the tines of one barely touching those of the next. And in the space formed between the handles I put the next row of forks. Perfection indeed. I wiped each piece dry and placed it on the counter. As I dried the last utensil, I found I had divided a clean dish towel into four neat sections and had placed salad forks in the upper right, dinner knives in the lower left. Spoons nestled in right below the forks, and, lined up in the upper left, the but-ter knives lay waiting to be put back into their velvet-lined case.

And as I was arranging the silverware at this party, in my mind I could very well have been arranging silverware at Blueberry Hill. Silverware arranging was the ideal job for me then since it kept me occupied for a half hour or so. And I was good at it too, always aware of the symmetry and tidiness, and always considerate of all the things that needed to go on the table for the buffet to be complete. I realized even then that my silverware arrangement was not the buffet focal point, but that it was important, and it was, moreover, worth taking the time to make a clean and tidy arrangement.

The dining room door opened and John came over and stood next to me as I drifted away with my silverware wiping. "Huh! That's pretty!" he said. "Do you always do that?" I made up some excuse about wanting the client to find her dishes well organized when she came into the kitchen, not letting on that I was enjoying this innocent and very personal time travel.

So, lately I think that what I am doing is exactly the right thing for me. I get to share my mother's foods with other people, I have the chance to create my own business, doing it exactly the way I want, and any time I want. And I just have to walk through my kitchen to be tucked into the smells and sounds and flavors of the place that I loved the best.

Chapter Thirty-Five

Refrigerator Doors

 My sisters and I keep track of each other by looking in our refrigerators—especially in the doors. Isn't the door the most interesting place to look?

In mine right now, there are three kinds of mustard: an extra hot, a spicy, and a sweet; capers, hot cherry peppers, and pickled *pepperoncini*; a nice collection of syrups: two kinds of raspberry maple syrup, a jar of birch syrup (from Alaskan birch trees!), and some Vermont-made maple syrup. I also have Branston pickle relish, mango chutney, and a bottle of teriyaki marinade. There is ketchup and some cocktail sauce, not to mention a jar of Bartlett pear caramel sauce, some toasted sesame oil, a couple of "store-bought" salad dressings (but don't tell anyone), a bottle of A1 sauce, and a six-year old bottle of very spicy barbecue sauce I don't use but which has a great label so I keep it around. Oh, and I have three different types of horseradish.

My sisters' refrigerator doors aren't that much different. And it always is the first place we go when we visit.

"Three jars of horseradish!" they exclaim, checking things out before they even unpack.

They laugh at my pickle collection that takes up an entire half of one shelf. Like baseball cards, perhaps—I'm happiest when I have a complete collection.

Last month, when they came to be with me for my birthday, Heather volunteered to make lunch. Lucinda and I worked on building a fenced-in yard for my puppy. I could hear Heather sizzling things, stirring things, opening jars, and setting the table.

"Lunch is ready!" she called, drawing us inside. She had prepared a refrigerator feast for us: Sautéed Potatoes, Grilled Cheese Sandwiches, a buffet of marinated pickles and peppers and canned vegetables. Oh, and slices of Chicken Baked in Wine. A feast, Heather's offering, composed of discoveries in my refrigerator and leftovers carried from Lucinda's kitchen in Kentucky.

Our refrigerators prompt stories.

"Remember the time we cooked for three days and made twenty-five dishes for Thanksgiving and your father-in-law came in and asked where the olives were? Olives? At Thanksgiving?"

"Where'd you find this mustard? This is just like the kind Elise Churchill put on those awful steamed hot dogs! Why would you want to keep *this* stuff around?"

"Brandy sauce! Yum!"

And they never let me forget one specific time when they visited. I had gone to work early, leaving them to sleep in and fend for themselves for the morning. My refrigerator was stocked well enough, I thought. But anyone who can have a six-year-old bottle of barbecue sauce might have other surprises too, as my sisters discovered.

"We decided to make omelets," they reported later, still laughing, when I returned from work. "So we pulled out some cheese and sour cream and onions and butter."

"And I got out the eggs," Lucinda related.

"I had everything chopped and the pan was hot and everything!" Heather continued.

"So I cracked the eggs—and they *exploded*!" Lucinda doubled over laughing. "They were so old there was nothing left but sulfur fumes. You are amazing! The expiration date was one whole year ago!"

I sat through this teasing, smiling at myself—and knowing it could easily happen again.

Chapter Thirty-Six

A Letter to My Sisters

Dear Lucinda and Heather,

Well, I rarely go into detail about parties, but since the one last night was so spectacular, I thought it might be fun for you to hear about one. It really was fabulous!

I met with the bride and groom about six months ago. She is from the eastern part of the state, near the ocean. His background seemed less important, but, to all of us, it did seem fitting to have the menu representative of the mountains, their chosen home, and the coast, a place dear to both of their hearts. Many of the guests were coming from the east and I quickly caught on that it would be good if we could impress them. The bride was the third and last daughter to be married, and the mother was clear about making sure she got as much attention as her sisters had.

I think we did it.

The biggest decision, as far as the bride and groom were concerned, was the cake. We made them a taste of four or five different types of our favorites, and invited them for breakfast one morning a few months ago. It was fun to give them each a cup of coffee and present them with a plate of fancy cupcakes. I left them alone to eat, but watched as they did. A bit voyeuristic, perhaps, but fun. They cooed at each other and it looked like they were really comparing and contrasting. They left without telling me what they wanted.

The menu was a different story. The couple was delighted with everything I came up with, being pleased with a "From the Mountains to the Sea" idea. We decided to have four main areas making up the meal: a presentation of assorted vegetable things, a pasta area, a meat area, and a seafood area.

"We trust whatever you do!" the bride and groom chirped.

The mother was quite a bit fussier, requesting a number of changes. I am very aware that when the big day comes, no one really has much of a clue about any of the foods that are being served, but clearly the process mattered very much to her, so I made the changes she requested. "Please add Brie" and "please let's not have *any* turkey!" "Do you think we need more salads?" "What about fruit?" We talked for at least two hours about the foods, going through the menu in excruciating detail, one item at a time.

"And how, exactly, do you *cut* the fruit?" she asked. "What kind of wood do you use to smoke the fish? And what exactly is 'salmon trout'?" and, "What do your serving utensils look like?"

"Cousin Louise" is vegetarian so we added Black Bean Cakes accompanied by Fresh Salsa and Sour Cream. The Mountains needed representation so I had suggested Trout, smoked in our back yard with Apple Wood chips. That made it onto the menu, but "The Men" would like meat (do the men really like meat or is it just that the women *think* men like meat? Maybe the *women* like meat but are scared to admit it!), so we filled in that section: Rack of Lamb, cooked in front of the guests; skewered Teriyaki Chicken with a Spicy Peanut Sauce; Tenderloin of Beef with a Horseradish Sauce; and an Herb-Crusted Ham, sliced and served with our own rolls and breads.

"Well," the mother hesitated, "I'm not so sure about the ham." Too plebian, I suspected? She couldn't define her concern, so I decided to try to talk her into the ham, knowing that the crowd needed some foods of substance, not just a bunch of fussy things. They would like our ham, I thought. "You will not be embarrassed!" I assured her, "It's really good! We'll make a thick herb crust with Dijon mustard and dark brown sugar. I'm sure you'll love it."

I was happy with my suggestions for the vegetable area, but we had recently won the Sweet Potato contest from Southern Foodways Alliance with Richard's incredible Roasted Sweet Potato Salad, so the mother asked to add it to the menu. We agreed on the "Southern Antipasto," which is becoming another of our specialties: roasted and marinated seasonal vegetables, cheeses, sometimes meats. On this menu we had baby carrots and local cukes, both pickled by us, and Richard's Oven Roasted Tomatoes (which are *really* good!) We also had a "Roasted Potato Bar" with Red Bliss and Yukon Gold Potato Wedges and a bunch of things for people to sprinkle on top. (Remember how Daddy used to scold, "Don't play with your food!"? I wonder what he'd think of all this?)

And there was a lot of conversation with the mother about the Pasta Station. I like Marinara the best, and Alfredo is a good second choice. I had to talk the mother out of Capellini or Fettuccine. I know what holds up and what doesn't, and what smells good and what doesn't. We went back and forth: "What about Pesto?" "Shall we do a Meat Sauce?" "I don't know, do you *like* Cheese Tortellini? What about Ravioli?" We ended up with what I

154

had suggested when I wrote the menu originally: Penne with Marinara and Roasted Vegetables, and Cheese Tortellini with an Alfredo Sauce.

The seafood area, in addition to the Smoked Trout, had Skewers of Shrimp and Pineapple with Lea's Soy and Garlic Marinade. It's *really* good and is different. "We don't want plain old shrimp cocktail!" the mother had emphasized. I sort of agree, but it *is* amazing that people *love* Shrimp with Cocktail Sauce, especially when you put it in a ice sculpture! (Last week I did a large party and served shrimp in a big rectangular box cut from ice. I brought John's Dunk Sauce instead of Cocktail Sauce. *Big* hit!) We also decided to have Sautéed Soft-Shell Crabs in this area.

The gang in the kitchen worked on this party for most of the day on Friday and all day Saturday. My biggest concern was when to finish cooking everything. We had three cooks scheduled to cook at the party: one for the pasta area, one for the meats, and one for the fish area. (By the way, I had never even met two of them before that night!) Now, you can't really cook all that food from scratch in front of 225 people. It just takes too long. It needs to be almost completely cooked, but, of course, not overcooked. I pondered and I fretted over the math and timing and cooking conundrum for much of the day, pacing and muttering to myself, "Okay, now if the lamb takes twenty minutes to cook but I want to finish cooking it at the party and we need to get it to the party in time to set it up and organize it *and* finish cooking it, I'll need to put it in the oven by six so I can take it out of the oven and get it carried to the party and finished cooking by six thirty. Right, the guests are coming at seven so that should work. But don't forget, you also have to cook the shrimp skewers, the chicken skewers, *and* the soft-shell crabs, not to mention having to heat up the bean cakes. If the shrimp takes fifteen minutes and the chicken takes twenty minutes and we only have ten shelves in the ovens and I've now used up twenty, which gets cooked first? And *when* do I think I should cook the crabs? And oh, um, how am I going to cook the crabs?" (I still hadn't decided exactly how I was going to cook that night's featured event!)

The funny things about all of this is that I go crazy trying to think about it and it is nearly impossible for me to describe a plan to someone, but I do have an inner "Cooking Guide" who, if I let it, will tell me *exactly* where to put what pan, when, and for how long.

As the hours ticked by during the day I turned the menu around and around in my mind: " . . . fifteen minutes at 350 and then turn the second batch of crabs . . . don't forget the capers . . . did I remember to ask for extra basil . . . ?"

And then, instinctively, I *knew* it was time. I went up to the kitchen, turned on the oven, the burners, the griddle, and started cooking. While the oil for the crabs was heating, I put in the chicken kebobs and got the shrimp and pineapple skewers ready. I also took the trays of Mustard-glazed Rack of Lamb from the walk-in and stirred up a batch of seasoned flour. I pulled out butter, lemons, capers, tongs, spatula, hot pads, and started to cook.

I had three large pans full of crabs, about 144 in all. And though I had had the idea of cooking them on the griddle, when I actually did it they just didn't cook very well. (You might wonder why I hadn't tried this before party time but I guess I like the adrenaline rush of this kind of last-minute "we'll see if *this* works" approach.) But I also had a big pan of oil heating up and so, even though that meant I could only cook fifteen at a time instead of forty at a time on the griddle, I resigned myself to it and dredged and started cooking the first pan full. I splashed them with white wine, tossed on some capers, and, happy with the result, flipped them over. Yup! This was going to work!

Time to check the skewers. They were cooking unevenly (this is why I am buying new ovens!) so I rotated them and went back to the crabs.

The first pan was done, so I lined them up in a clean pan and started in on the second batch. The staff for the party came to collect all the other food (did I mention that the party was just down the street, making it *very* convenient?). My cooks arrived and I sent them down to scope out the location. I had already described everything to Bronwen, one of our part-time cooks and one of the three who was cooking that night, so she took the other two on their field trip. When they came back, I got them going on prepping garnishes—busy-work, but necessary: chopping parsley, chiffonnading basil (cutting it into thin strips), collecting the final cooking utensils and condiments.

Meanwhile the first batch of skewers was done and Bronwen took over, rotating, stacking, transferring skewers to "aluminum boys," the pans we send to parties. Kelly and Keith chopped; I sautéed more crabs.

"We have thirty minutes until the guests come," Karen, the party director breezed through. She'd spent almost the entire day setting tables, arranging buffets, flowers, linens, cooking areas. She scurried off to change into her party clothes. "I'll be right back and I'll take more food with me!" she said.

I sent the three cooks to the party with the rest of the skewers and the bean cakes. It was now time for them to get their stations set up. Keith was cooking pasta and his area had the two types of pasta, two sauces, roasted vegetables, two cooking burners, two saucepans, and lots of back-up of all his condiments and ingredients.

Bronwen got her lamb-sautéing area going and also heated up her grill for the chicken. Kelly got some garlic sizzling and splashed in some wine which made the whole club smell great. (Nothing like a sizzle of garlic to set the stage for a party!) She started to finish the first pan of Soft-Shell Crabs that I'd par-cooked.

By then I had finished two of the three pans of crabs and had decided to take the lamb out of the oven before 20 minutes was up. "They'll be too rare!" the worrier on my left shoulder scolded. "No they won't, they'll be perfect!" the guide on my right soothed.

I packed up three large pans full of lamb racks ("I hope you're right!") and sent them off.

I finished up the last four batches of crabs, packed them into a pan, skipped downstairs, changed clothes, grabbed my camera, came back upstairs, got the crabs, and carried them down to the club.

Everything was *almost* ready, but the lighting designer was suddenly absent. We had five minutes before the guests were to arrive, and the work lights were still on! I needed to finish my little bit of lighting that I had brought (we rigged up some little portable pin spots to highlight individual platters) so we scrambled around, found the lighting guy, got the work lights off, focused the lights, did some final touches, and took a whole roll of pictures—*quickly!*—just before the first guests arrived!

So, from then on it was smooth and fine. Everything looked beautiful! Karen had rented shiny bright blue, purple, red, gold, green, pink, and orange fabrics which popped in the club's light. We'd tied a bright ribbon on each black (yes!) napkin and the colors danced and vibrated. To present the foods we used our galvanized trays and mixed them in with glass platters, terra cotta plates, and a few baskets. Karen dragged in our old rusty tin ceiling pieces and weathered barn boards too. I used our old wooden divider screens as lighting positions, and spot lit the trout, the crabs, the pasta. They had asked for "eclectic." They got it!

When the guests arrived they squealed with pleasure. The mom and dad seemed pleased, and the bride and groom were speechless.

The finale was the cake, of course. In the end, the bride and groom had settled on alternating layers of white cake with a raspberry filling and lemon poppy seed with a lemon curd filling. The whole cake was covered in buttercream with little white dots that looked like pearls arranged symmetrically, cascading down the cake from layer to layer. Karen draped real flowers in a spiral of deep fall colors. It was gorgeous! And the groom's cake was Carrot and had a little Mexican Day of the Dead statue on top. We had carved steps in the piled square cake so it look like a tiny old Mayan pyramid. Very cute.

It really was the nicest party I've ever seen. You would have been amazed. But boy, was I tired!

And, as I always do after a party like this, I went home, had a bowl of cereal, and watched stupid TV until I could stop seeing crabs in my head.

I love you both,

PQ

Chapter Thirty-Seven

A Red Table

Today I fell in love with a red table. This table, rusty and old and battered, has rickety old dinged-up yellow legs. I saw it at a store just two days ago and today I went and bought it for the new shop I am building. I took Emily, from my office, with me because I broke a rib two weeks ago when I fell off a horse at my sister Lucinda's house, and I really am not supposed to be picking things up just yet. I keep forgetting and picking things up anyway, but Emily watches out for me, and when we got to the store she said, "Don't you let me catch you picking up that table" in a voice that made me drop my hands to my sides and let her pick up whatever it is without any help.

I also bought four red chairs, four ratty old galvanized rectangular baskets, and then, on my way out the door, a blue chair and a yellow chair. All the chairs are those Parisian "bistro" chairs that you see all over the place in that lovely city. They have so many chairs in Paris, two under almost every tree in almost every park. The last time I was there I realized that I never see any chains locking these tables in place. I never notice any locks or cables or anything that would prevent someone from just walking away with them. Paris is a different sort of place.

Emily loaded my new chairs into my car and we drove them back to work, stopping in a vacant space right in front of my new shop. "Parking karma," I mutter to myself. As I started to open the back door of my car, Emily glared at me, which made me stop what I was doing and watch her. It is way too easy to forget that I need to be careful. This is the vulnerable time, I'm told. Now is when I need to be especially careful not to bump into something or pick up an object that is too heavy. My rib is just barely knitted together and I could easily rebreak it. I stand aside and let Emily carry everything into the shop.

Woody, the carpenter, is working on the framework for the wall in my new shop that will separate the kitchen from the public space. There are three distinct holes in the new wall, where new windows will go. I've been doing a lot of shopping lately and earlier this week I bought three matching faded old windows with chipped yellow paint on their frames. I fell in love with these windows just the other day and now they rest on the floor of the new shop, waiting to be put into the holes that Woody has framed in the new wall he's building. I've been imagining window boxes with bright red geraniums or lush little ferns underneath real windows. My vision is becoming reality.

There is a quiet comfort in these simple purchases as I begin to feel that this new space is going to be mine. A reflection of me. And now, with my little red table and my four red and one blue and one yellow chairs, not to mention the three yellow windows, it is beginning to take shape.

Both of my previous kitchens were considerate places. "Do you think this table looks good here?" I've asked politely. Or, "What color paint do you think would be best?" I have a design background but I've pushed it aside as I've tried to include everyone.

I've had my own opinions, but I've never really let them out so overtly before. This time, however, this project, this kitchen really feels different to me. I'm still being pretty intentional about including everyone. And I really do care what they think. They are, after all, the people who will be working in the new space. But my questions are more practical. "Do you think fifteen feet is a big enough walk-in cooler?" I ask. Or, "Do you think this is a good spot for the coffee service?" But while I ask these questions, I feel a significant shift deep inside me. I consult and I include and I consider the group sentiment, but this place, I realize, will be, at its heart, a reflection of me and of what I think is good. And this, I realize, is not the way I've ever done it before.

So today I fell in love with a little red table and some chairs and I came back and set them up and then stood back, admiring and smiling. Ignoring my sore rib, and avoiding Emily, I dragged the big red outdoor umbrella over and raised it up so that it hovered over my newest heart throb, sheltering it from dust and nails and such.

I might, I think, just make myself a picnic one night, pack it in a basket and take it into work, let myself in, and sit at my little red table under my red umbrella and watch the world drive up and down in front of my new shop. The moon, I think, rises just over the mountains in front of the shop window. I'll sit there until the moon rises, I decide.

Champagne might be nice, though if you want to know the truth, a peanut butter sandwich and a big glass of milk would be just as good. Maybe even better. Yup. I'll sit on one of my new red chairs and watch the moon rise. It's a good and simple thing to fall in love with a little red and yellow table and a couple of faded old chairs.

Chapter Thirty-Eight

The Great Blue Heron

 The first time I ever saw a Blue Heron was at Blueberry Hill very early one morning. I saw it about three minutes after I realized My Maple Tree had blown down. Just the day before, the tree had been standing, tired, old, and almost completely branchless, but still upright.

I had left New York for a weekend and, after being away from Vermont for years, I had returned to Goshen and had spent the day wandering around my old land. I had ended up standing under the scrap of the old Maple Tree that remained standing. Tony, the new owner of Blueberry Hill, and I talked.

"She won't last much longer," he'd said, referring to my Tree.

"But you'll never cut it, will you? Promise me, okay?" I'd said.

"I feel like that tree brought me up," I explained. "I spied on guests from a spot in those branches. I threw things at my sisters, watched cars driving up and down the road, and just climbed up into its notch and read a book sometimes. I'd hate to see it chopped down, even if it is about to go."

I thought of my parents: the time my mother came out of the kitchen to scold me for the incessant drumming I was doing on the floor of my treehouse with my new drumsticks. And the time when I was eight, and my father had caught me practicing really shifting the gears on our Citroën, parked right under the Maple's branches.

"Don't worry," Tony soothed. "I'll never cut it."

But that night, a huge wind had blasted across the fields from way over on the western side of Lake Champlain. The gusts had come from miles and miles away, all the way in New York State. My Maple, the first thing in the wind's path, got knocked over like a twig. In the morning, out for a walk by myself, I saw my tree, strewn, its branches a skeleton of broken chips laid out in the wet grass.

"You waited for me," I thought. "You waited for me to come home before you gave up."

Now of course by then I was many years too big for tree climbing, but seeing my tree smashed into the ground made me feel as if a part of me, a part of my history, had fallen and broken into pieces during that storm. I picked up a knotty chunk of wood.

Clutching my chunk, I padded across the dirt road into the apple orchard, past the blueberry bushes and ended up, without having paid much attention, at Daddy's pond. This was the pond that he had planned and we'd started building that summer when he was so sick. He'd be pleased, I thought. He'd have liked this pond. My mother would have been proud of herself for taking on the project alone. Yes, they would both have been happy to see this pond on a morning like this.

That morning, the surface of the pond was smooth, and clearly reflected the beginning of the dawn, the trees, and the foggy wisps of morning. Even though we were close to the Inn, it was still too early for anyone to be awake. I was completely alone. Everything was absolutely still.

Suddenly, I saw a pair of Great Blue Herons reflected in the surface of the pond. Lifting my head, I watched as two beautiful birds flew up over the water, circled the pond, dipped in toward me, and then slowly, quietly flew off to the north. And, in a breath, they were gone.

Still alone, I realized with absolute clarity that these birds were my parents, doing a final salute: a salute to the Inn, to the pond, to the tree, and, perhaps, to me, too. In all the time I'd lived in Vermont I'd never seen one Blue Heron. But yet, there they were, a pair of them, seen just by me.

In that moment it seemed as if they were saying, "We're here. We're still with you. We're looking out for you. We saw the tree. We know. This visit is to let you know that we're here for you if you ever need us."

I shook my head, dazed by these thoughts. I was not someone who found this kind of meaning in this kind of thing. Usually if I saw a bird, it just seemed that I'd, well, seen a bird. But that morning was different. I was certain I'd had a visit from another place.

It turns out that that morning was the only time I'd ever see a pair of Blue Herons flying together. But it was just the beginning of a long string of visits I've had from a single glorious bird. The visits have become markers for me; times when I have needed a special nudge of comfort, a sign letting me know I am on the right track.

For a long time, I'd see a Great Blue Heron on the first day of an important trip. One flew across the bow of my canoe on the first day of a big trip in Canada one year. And once, on the first day of training for a long bike ride, a Heron traveled with me, flying ahead and around a bend in the road, waiting for me to catch up, and then taking off again.

"I'm here. I'm with you. You can do this," it seemed to say.

And after that first time at the pond, a Blue Heron often appeared when an important moment came in my life. On the first day of my first business trip to Italy, a Heron flew across the highway right over my car. In Italy!

"I'm with you. You can do this."

And then, on the last day, after the trip was done, in almost the same place on the same highway, the Blue Heron flew back.

"See, I knew you could," I heard.

The Heron shows up in other ways too. One time, rehearsing for a difficult theatre piece, I saw in a corner of the rehearsal studio a corner of a print of—yes—a Great Blue Heron. This theatre piece, a challenging and very personal performance about my mother, had become increasingly harder to do. Was it too much to be this open in public, I wondered?

"I'm with you. You can do this," the picture whispered. I continued to rehearse, feeling comforted by the message. (Later, after the performance, when I told the studio's owner about the significance of Herons, he gave me the print, which now hangs in my kitchen at my home.)

There have even been times when my Heron visitor shows a sense of humor. On a ski trip out west, aware that all of my trips in the past few years had started and ended with a Blue Heron sighting, I looked up from a plate of New Mexican tacos at a restaurant near the airport where I had gone to have lunch and wait for lost luggage, and there, in front of the restaurant window, appeared a U-Haul truck with—yup—a Blue Heron painted on its side. Cute, I thought, smiling. Very cute.

Recently, I went through a time of personal darkness. I struggled with decisions, tried to find answers, and began searching for some help. I found myself actively looking for the Blue Heron.

"Where *are* you?" I heard myself saying. "Where are you now, when I need you to tell me if I am okay, if I can do *this*? Why don't you fly across my car *now*?"

But I did not see any Herons. I searched and thought and gradually began to edge out into a lighter place. And then, just when I'd forgotten all about the Heron, it appeared, though in a completely new way.

My dog and I were on a hike in the woods near town here. Coming around a bend, we saw a white-haired woman, off, I assumed, for a walk, too. I waved but, not feeling conversational, kept walking. My dog and I hiked up the hill, around the top of the hiking area, and made our way back to the parking lot. And at the end of our walk, just before I put my pup into my car, I noticed the woman again.

This time, something made me stop, let her catch up, and say hello.

"What a beautiful day," she chirped. "I'm so glad it stopped raining."

"Me too," I agreed.

"And aren't we fortunate to have these woods for our walks?" she continued. "I love these woods, but I also love the lake. I alternate my walking between up here in the woods and down around the lake."

"Mmm hmm," I nodded. She seemed pleasant enough. But why did I feel compelled to talk to her? She was just a regular older woman, right?

"I haven't seen any Great Blue Herons in a long time," she muttered, clear out of the blue. (We had not been talking about birds or Herons, after all.) "But," she continued, "sometimes they just need to go away for a time. They always do come back, though. Well, it has been nice talking with you."

And over the hill she flew.

I stood, dazed as she disappeared.

"I'm still here," I heard. "And you, my child, will be fine."

Chapter Thirty-Nine

Elsie's Biscuits

 My hands now make my mother's biscuits. And when they do, it is as if she is inside me, guiding my hands, making me move. It is a remarkable and comforting thing. I know, of course, that they are my hands, but when I look down, they could very well be hers. I was with her so much then. I saw her make so many many biscuits.

Her hands, like mine now, were a bit puffy. Whenever she made biscuits, which was every single night at the Inn, she first removed her wedding ring and hung it on a nail on the upright support at the side of the faded yellow work counter which my father had built for her when they were just getting started with the Inn and couldn't afford to hire anyone else to build anything. It was not a perfect counter. It was very homemade, but it worked well enough and it had been made with love and it had a nail just to hold her ring while she made biscuits.

I waited quietly on the other side, watching, patient and so very happy.

In she'd plunge.

I can still see her mixing the margarine into a bowl filled with her measured flour, baking powder, and salt. She used the two-knife method to blend, passing two simple table knives with strong, sure strokes *fwicking* against each other. *Click. Whick.* Smoothly past each other. Slice the sticks of margarine in two. In four. In eight and smaller and smaller until it was, as she said, "the consistency of corn snow," blended and mixed until it looked like tiny kernels of flour. She could have used one of those pastry tools, the ones with a wooden handle and the wires that curve like a big letter U. She could have used her hands, the way I have seen folks here do, southerners for the most part, crumbling the flour into the margarine with their fingers. Mostly I think people follow the way they learned from their mothers and grandmothers. My mother learned from her mother. My mother, I remember, used the two-knife method, so I do too.

I loved to watch her.

Once she had a bowl of "corn snow" flour, she poured in the combined milk, buttermilk, and, to make the biscuits really light, sour cream. She stirred with a wooden spoon just until the instant when the mixture held together. Mix them too much, I knew, and the biscuits would be tough. Too little and they'd fall apart. My mother, after who knows how many hundreds and hundreds of times of making biscuits, knew exactly when to stop.

She coaxed the sticky dough onto her pastry board, a wooden board inlaid by my father into the surface of her work counter. She'd coated the board with flour first and then had dusted a bit more flour on top of the doughy pile, gently patting, shaping, and forming the mass into the thickness that would produce, she knew, the perfect biscuits.

I squirmed, getting ready. My moment was almost here.

As she tucked and worked and eased the dough into shape, I readied my baking sheet and got myself all set to help. She'd dip her biscuit cutter, really just a piece of smoothed aluminum cocoa butter tube (my sister reminded me this is what she used, though I'd always thought it was a piece of pipe) which my father had made especially for her biscuits, into a cup of flour and cut out one pipe-wide biscuit, and then shake it out of the pipe onto the board near my hand where it landed with a fat little plop. Dip. Cut. Shake. Plop. Dip. Cut. Shake. Plop. Dip. Cut. Shake. Plop.

Finally it was time for me!

Staying clear of the pipe and clear of my mother's swift hands, I lined up the little biscuit cutouts on my baking tray. I was precise, making long, straight rows of biscuits down and across my sheet, thrilled, every night, to be a part. I grinned, catching my mother's eye. I was a big help, I could see!

My mother popped my baking sheet into her oven as the guests, now finished with their Shrimp Tempura with John's Dunk Sauce, followed my father through the kitchen and into the dining room. As they sat down and ate Prosciutto wrapped around wedges of summer-ripe Cantaloupe, the biscuits puffed in the oven and, just as my mother gave the Blueberry Hill Salad its final toss, were done. Scooted off the tray and tucked into a Blue Willow napkin-lined basket and served with that summer's Blueberry Jam, my mother's biscuits were perfect steaming bite-size puffs.

If I sat very quietly, I could stay next to my mother's counter for a long time, past my bedtime on many occasions, and almost always long enough to get a couple of back-from-the-dining-room, still-warm, biscuits. My mother's biscuits. Made by her. And me.

That was then. Now I do it all. Just me. I measure, mix, pat, scrape, coax, flour, cut, shake, and line up. And then I bake and serve. Just me. Just me and my mother's hands. Just us.

Elsie's Biscuits
The Recipe

Here's another classic recipe—at least for me and the thousands of people who ate at my parents' Blueberry Hill or who have been to one of my many catered events. We make a bazillion of these things each year. Sometimes we add grated Vermont Cheddar Cheese and Fresh Dill, which makes a delicious foundation for a savory hors d'oeuvre like a Maple-Glazed Ham Biscuit. And sometimes we make them a bit bigger than normal, sprinkle some sugar and cinnamon on top, split them, fill them with fresh fruit and whipped cream, and call them Shortcake. But, truthfully, they are so wonderful just plain that I almost hesitate to even suggest these variations to you.

Here's my mother's recipe.

This recipe will make enough biscuits for about 8 people: 30 little biscuits, or 15 medium-sized ones, or 8 big guys.

The ingredients:

3 cups all-purpose flour
2 tablespoons baking powder
1 teaspoon table salt
$1/4$ pound margarine (1 stick)
$1/2$ cup milk (you might need a little more)

$1/2$ cup buttermilk
$1/3$ cup sour cream
$1/8$ teaspoon vanilla
$1/8$ teaspoon sugar

Here's what you do: Sift the flour with the baking powder and salt. With two knives or a pastry blender, cut in the margarine. When all lumps are eliminated (it should look like corn meal), add milk, buttermilk, sour cream, vanilla, and sugar. Stir only until combined. Add a little more milk if it isn't quite a wet dough.

Toss the dough in a little flour until you can handle it. Pat it down gently with floured hands. Do not roll it. When it is about $1/2$ inch thick, cut out the biscuits. Place them carefully on a lightly greased baking sheet. (If you have a little girl around, let her line them up for you, why don't you?)

Bake for 12 minutes in a hot (450–500°F) conventional oven. The temperature will depend on your oven, of course. Some run hot, some run cool. And convection ovens will make the whole thing go much faster, you know. You will, I hope, have a feel for yours. And, if your biscuits are very small, say $\frac{1}{2}$ inch in diameter, they'll cook in just a few minutes: 5 to 7, let's say. But if you're making larger fellows, 3 to 4 inches, for example, you'll probably be looking at 10+ minutes. Keep an eye on them and you'll be fine. Look for a light golden tinge to the very top of each biscuit. Then you'll know they are ready.

Oh, they are incredible if you can manage to cook them right before you want to serve them. And yes, they do freeze and reheat, but the right-out-of-the-oven sensation is unbeatable. I love them with a little bit of butter and a spoonful of fresh jam.

Enjoy!

Chapter Forty

Where We Are Now

Twenty years after starting in my tiny upstairs apartment, I now have a thriving business with three distinct parts:

One part is off-premise parties: weddings, bar mitzvahs, benefits, fancy dinners, celebrations of all kinds. For these we assemble everything and then pack it up and haul it off to a nearby mountaintop or park or back yard or field where we put on simple and elaborate events. We're getting better at avoiding the disasters, but still collect tales of events that have a story to tell.

Another part of my current business consists of dropped-off parties: business lunches, family gatherings—events with no service, just food. These are a good piece of the work these days, but generally don't have much to report. We make the food. We take it someplace. We drop it off. Later we go back and pick up empty dishes and baskets. That's about it.

The third part of my business is the "shop" (as I say) or "the café" (as others sometimes call it), which is a large, airy space filled with seating tables. Guests come in, choose from an array of freshly-made salads from our packed deli case. We have hot specials in the winter, chilled things in hotter months. I've starting calling it "gourmet comfort food." A whole team of cooks flutters about the kitchen, carving up boxes of fresh produce and local ingredients. Periodically someone from someplace else will come to Asheville and write about our town and, sometimes, this shop. Then, when the story comes out, more people come for lunch. I like it. "Coming to Asheville? Come to Laurey's!"

Things have come a long way from the days when it was just me working out of my tiny walk-up apartment. Asheville is a good place to be. My street, the heart of the downtown renaissance, is a bustling place and I'm very happy that things have turned out this way. Blueberry Hill would have been nice. And I still miss it. But this, for me, is just fine.

I thought I'd finish this particular book by including a favorite recipe from each of the cooks. After a few years of ruining things in the kitchen, I decided to stop cooking. I was finding myself in more and more meetings with clients and, well, I was realizing that I was not a very reliable worker. The team behind the stoves is terrific. They are a creative bunch, loyal and happy (almost all of the time, that is). And while each of them can make just about anything, each one has something that is especially their creation. They've all agreed to share that special recipe with you. Here goes.

Deb's Crab Cakes

Though these started out as *my* crab cakes, they have become Deb's signature. She has tweaked the recipe and it is the one we all turn to now. When she's not cooking she can be found making beautiful watercolors (especially of peonies), playing classical guitar, or singing with the local symphony chorus.

This recipe will make enough crab cakes for 20 dinner-size crab cakes—easily enough for 12 people. As you might guess, it'll make a whole lot more if you make the smaller ones.

Serves 12

The ingredients:

1 pound claw crabmeat
6 cups soft bread crumbs (make by
     pulsing slightly stale bread in
     the food processor)
1/2 cup diced red bell pepper
1/2 cup diced yellow bell pepper
3/4 cup diced red onion
1/4 cup chopped fresh parsley
1 tablespoon Dijon mustard

2 tablespoons fresh lemon juice
1/4 teaspoon Tabasco sauce
1/4 cup freshly grated Parmesan cheese
1/4 cup drained capers
2 cups mayonnaise
Olive oil or seasoned oil, or seasoned
     pan coating spray
Herbed sour cream, for serving (optional)

Here's what you do: Preheat the oven to 350°F. Line a baking sheet (8 x 13 x 1) with parchment paper.

Combine the crabmeat, 4 cups of the bread crumbs, the red and yellow peppers, onion, parsley, mustard, lemon juice, Tabasco, Parmesan, capers, and mustard in a large bowl.

The mixture should hold together, but not be too wet or too dry. Add more bread crumbs or mayonnaise if necessary. Put the remaining bread crumbs in a shallow dish or on a piece of parchment paper on a flat surface.

Scoop the crab mixture onto the parchment paper-lined tray with an ice cream scoop (we use various sizes, depending on if we are making hors d'oeuvres or dinner-size cakes).

Flatten each crab cake with a pancake turner. Gently roll each cake in the remaining bread crumbs to coat on all sides, and put on the baking sheet.

Spritz with olive oil or seasoned oil. You can also use seasoned pan coating spray if you wish.

Bake at 350°F for 12 to 20 minutes, depending on the size of the cake. They are done when the breading is lightly toasted.

If you like, serve with a bit of herbed sour cream.

Note: The crab cakes can be made ahead of time and kept in the refrigerator until mealtime. When ready to cook, spritz with oil and bake as instructed. You can also bake them ahead of time and reheat them, but they are better when baked right before eating.

Martha's Black Bean Cakes

Martha has been with us for quite some time now. She was one of the cooks at Irregardless—a restaurant in Raleigh that was named that because the owner's English teacher had once told him that was *not* a real word; after he named his restaurant that, it became one.

Martha is in charge of our Dinner-To-Go menu, which means that every month she has to decide what we will be offering for the entire next month. Yes, she includes the other cooks, but it is primarily her responsibility.

This is one of her inventions, one of her favorites. She often makes a simple salsa to go along with them. Mango and pineapple and tomatoes with some lime juice and some cilantro would be a good option. Enjoy!

Makes 10 cakes

The ingredients:

Olive oil
1 cup chopped yellow onion
1 ½ teaspoons minced garlic
1 ½ teaspoons ground cumin
¾ cup grated carrots (about 4 whole,
    medium-size carrots)
2 ½ cups cooked black beans,
    rinsed and drained

¼ teaspoon cayenne pepper
¼ cup Tahini
⅓ cup chopped parsley
⅓ cup all-purpose flour
¾ teaspoon baking soda
1 ½ teaspoons kosher salt
Toasted sesame seeds
Paprika

Here's what you do: Line a baking sheet (8 x 13 x 1) with parchment paper and brush the paper with olive oil or spray with pan spray. Preheat the oven to 400°F.

In a medium skillet, sauté the onion in ¼ cup olive oil until soft and transparent—about 5 minutes. Add the garlic and cumin and sauté for 2 more minutes. Add the carrots and sauté for 2 more minutes.

In a large bowl, toss the cooked vegetables with the black beans. Pulse in a food processor until mixed but still chunky. Using a spoon, gently mix the cayenne and the Tahini into bean mixture. Finally, fold in the parsley.

In a small bowl, whisk together the flour, baking soda, and salt. Add the flour mixture to bean mixture and mix in gently.

Scoop ⅓-cup portions of the bean mixture onto the baking sheet. Flatten the cakes with a fork and sprinkle with toasted sesame seeds and paprika.

Bake at 400°F for 15 minutes, or until golden brown.

Serve warm or at room temperature, accompanied by salsa if you like.

Kether's Israeli Couscous Salad

I met Kether when she was a student at our local culinary school. Through a professional association, Women Chefs and Restaurateurs, I became her mentor, which meant that I was able to follow her progress as she completed school, searched for what to do, moved to Atlanta, worked for a country club, got disillusioned, and, ultimately moved back to Asheville.

A year or so later I found myself at a tricky place in my business. All of a sudden we were very busy and, as happens in the world of food, I was short-staffed. One afternoon I bumped into her at a local restaurant.

"Are you back? Are you employed?" I asked. "We need someone! Would you like to come and cook with me—at least until you find something else?"

She agreed to come help us out until she found something else to do. I'm delighted to say that she's been here ever since.

Kether brings a delightful sense of taste and flavor to us. And she's terrific at creating meals and salads and accompaniments. Many of her additions are now a regular part of the deli case's contents. This is one of my favorites.

Serves 15

The ingredients:

3 cups Israeli couscous (see Note)
1/4 cup plus 1 tablespoon olive oil
1/2 tablespoon tomato paste
1/2 cup dried cherries, plus more
   for garnish
1/2 bunch scallions, cut on the diagonal—
   use the white and the green parts

1 orange
1 fresh, medium-size tomato, diced
   (no need to peel them)
Salt, freshly ground pepper, and
   Tabasco sauce
Chopped parsley, for garnish

Here's what you do: Mix the couscous with 1 tablespoon of the olive oil and toast over medium heat in a large saucepan until the grains are golden colored. This will take about 5 minutes over medium heat. (Be careful not to let the grains burn!)

Add 3 cups water and the tomato paste to the couscous. Stir in quickly and immediately cover with tight-fitting lid. Leave covered (no peeking!) on low heat for 10 minutes. Turn off the heat and leave untouched for 10 more minutes. Once couscous is cooked, turn it into large bowl and allow to cool to room temperature.

Grate the orange zest and set aside. Carefully cut the remaining white part off the orange. Working over a medium bowl to catch the juice, cut the orange segments out of the membrane and set them aside in a small bowl. Squeeze the juice out of the white part and the membrane into the bowl with the caught juice.

Stir the dried cherries, green onions, orange segments, and diced tomato into the couscous. Season to taste with salt, pepper, and Tabasco. Add the orange juice, orange zest, and the remaining ¼ cup olive oil. Toss well.

To serve, garnish with chopped parsley and more dried cherries.

This salad will keep for a day or two and will absorb the flavors over time. If you have other fresh vegetables or herbs, there is room for improvisation.

Note: Israeli couscous, a large-size pasta, can be found in health food stores and nicer grocery stores. Look in the dried pasta and rice sections.

Richard's Sweet Potato Salad

If there is a "Most Popular" recipe here at Laurey's, this is certainly it.

A few years ago, Richard, our head chef, was attempting to make Sweet Potato Chips. He'd sliced a tray full of potatoes, stuck them in the oven and then, in a lapse of attention, had forgotten about them. When he finally remembered, the chips had gotten singed and were, in his eyes, ruined.

However, on the way to the compost bin, he absent-mindedly tasted one. (Cooks are like that!) Hmm . . . they weren't bad! He slid the charred chips into a bowl, added some sourwood honey, a roasted onion, and some seasonings, and—a legend was born.

Richard's creation won first place at the Southern Foodways Alliance's "North Carolina Sweet Potato Cook-off" that was held in Asheville a few years ago. Fancy chefs from all the eating establishments around here brought intricate sweet potato dishes of all kinds: soufflés and gumbos and puffed this and meringued that. Theirs were good, but when it came time for the audience vote, Richard's won by unanimous uproar.

We now make pounds and pounds of this every day. And every time we serve it on a fancy party, I get e-mails and phone calls and letters requesting the recipe. Here it is for you to try.

Serves 4

The ingredients:

2 $\frac{1}{4}$ pounds North Carolina Sweet Potatoes (we grow more here in North Carolina than anywhere else in the entire world. Try to find ones from here. That'll be the most authentic way of making this recipe.)

1 medium red onion

1 teaspoon kosher salt

1 teaspoon freshly ground black pepper

1 teaspoon granulated garlic (not garlic salt, and not garlic powder)

$\frac{3}{4}$ cup olive oil

1 tablespoon Sourwood Honey (this unusual honey is another North Carolina product. If you can't find it, call me and I'll send some to you)

Juice of $\frac{1}{2}$ lemon

$\frac{1}{3}$ cup chopped fresh parsley

Here's what you do: Preheat a convection oven to 350°F (see Note). Line a large baking sheet with parchment paper.

Peel and quarter the sweet potatoes and red onion. Slice approximately ⅛-inch thick in a food processor.

Mix the potatoes and onion in a large bowl. Toss with the salt, pepper, garlic, and ½ cup of the oil (you'll need just enough oil to coat the potatoes—not more).

Spread the mixture on the baking sheet. Bake at 350°F, turning once, until the potatoes at the edge of the pan are quite brown. This will take about 20 minutes. Keep an eye on them. Try not to burn them, though the charring on the edges is my favorite part.

Allow to cool for 10 minutes.

Whisk together the honey, lemon juice, and the remaining ¼ cup olive oil in a clean large bowl. Add the cooked potato mixture and the chopped parsley. Combine gently. Serve.

We eat this at room temperature. I've heard of people having it hot, but I think that's not necessary.

Note: A convection oven is essential to this recipe as you want the sugars to burn, and that doesn't happen nearly as well in a conventional oven. In a pinch I have made it in a conventional oven and, yes, even in a cast-iron pan on the top of the stove, but to get the real result, I recommend using a convection oven—or coming to our shop and buying some that Richard made.

Adam's Sesame-Ginger Salad Dressing

We have such a varied and talented group! Adam is a DJ and a radio show host, and is a composer in the evenings. By day he is our shop manager, ably running the front of the house here. I know he is an accomplished cook, too, though that is not his primary job. Emily, our office manager, is married to him and I hear about their dinners a lot. Adam knows how to cook!

This is one of the recipes he brought to us. One time we catered meals for Bob Dylan when he came through town. The venue was right down the street from the shop at a great hall called The Orange Peel.

About a week after the concert we got a call from "the road." Bob Dylan's tour manager was on the phone, requesting the recipe for Adam's creation. We promptly typed it up and sent it off. We keep Adam's dressing in stock at all times. Bob, it turns out, is not the only one who loves it.

Here is Adam's recipe.

Makes 2 cups

The ingredients:

½ cup Tahini
6 tablespoons rice vinegar
3 tablespoons soy sauce
½ tablespoon granulated garlic
(again, not garlic salt, and not garlic powder)

½ tablespoon pureed ginger
(you can buy this in jars where Asian groceries are sold)
1 tablespoon sesame oil
⅓ cup olive oil

Here's what you do: Put the Tahini, vinegar, soy sauce, garlic, and ginger in a food processor and pulse until well combined. With the motor running, slowly add the sesame oil, olive oil, and 1 tablespoon water until the dressing thickens.

This salad dressing will keep well if you put the remainder in a container and refrigerate it. Shake well before serving.

Andrew's Portobello Wellington

Andrew is one of the shop gang. He epitomizes our wish to have a staff of "talented and interesting individuals." He has a band, he is helping raise two teenage boys, he grew up in Japan and speaks that language fluently. He's a gardener, a record collector, a jack of a number of trades—and he can cook! Here's one of his creations.

Serves 6.

The ingredients:

1 tablespoon minced garlic
1/4 pound butter (1 stick)
6 large Portobello mushroom caps
1/2 cup freshly grated Parmesan cheese
1/2 cup fresh Mozzarella, diced
1 large fresh tomato, seeded and diced

1/2 cup thin rings from a medium-size
    red onion
1/4 cup chopped fresh basil
Salt and freshly ground pepper
2 sheets frozen puff pastry, thawed
1 egg

Here's what you do: Preheat the oven to 350ºF. Line a baking sheet with parchment paper.

Combine the garlic and butter in a small saucepan and cook over low heat until the garlic becomes light golden brown.

Liberally brush the garlic butter on the underside of the mushroom caps. Place 2 or 3 onion rings on each cap followed by diced tomato, basil, Mozzarella, and Parmesan. Let stand for 2 to 3 minutes, so the butter can soak into the mushroom. Season with salt and pepper to taste.

Cut the pastry dough into 6 equal pieces. Place one cap in the center of a piece of dough and fold the corners over to completely envelop the cap.

Beat the egg with 1 tablespoon water and brush each finished mushroom packet on all sides with this "egg wash." Place on the baking sheet. Make sure the folded side of the pastry packets is facing up. Poke several small holes in the pastry.

Bake at 350°F for 20 to 25 minutes, until pastry crust is golden brown.

Enjoy!